I0819205

Beloved chef and two-time *Top Chef* Fan Favorite Sheldon Simeon's food joyfully reflects Hawai'i's flavors and cooking styles, a mixture of the islands' many cultures, including Native Hawaiian, Filipino, Japanese, Chinese, Korean, and Portuguese, among others. Sheldon's recipes blend sweet, savory, and tangy flavors into everyday meals, all the while keeping the traditions of family and communal-style eating at their heart.

With creative plant-based spins (like swapping out raw fish for pan-seared avocado for a delicious "tataki" or using mushrooms to create the best "escargot") and shortcut cooking techniques (like searing shoyu-marinated tuna in a hot pan to mimic smoking or using a Chinese dry wok cooking style for perfect fishsticks), the recipes in *Ohana Style* show how quick, easy, and flexible Hawaii cuisine can be.

OHANA STYLE

FOOD FROM HAWAI'I, FOR YOUR FAMILY

CLARKSON POTTER/PUBLISHERS NEW YORK

SHELDON SIMEON

OHANA

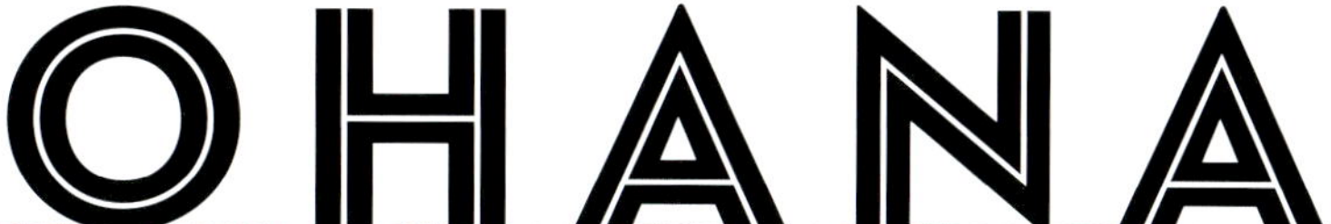

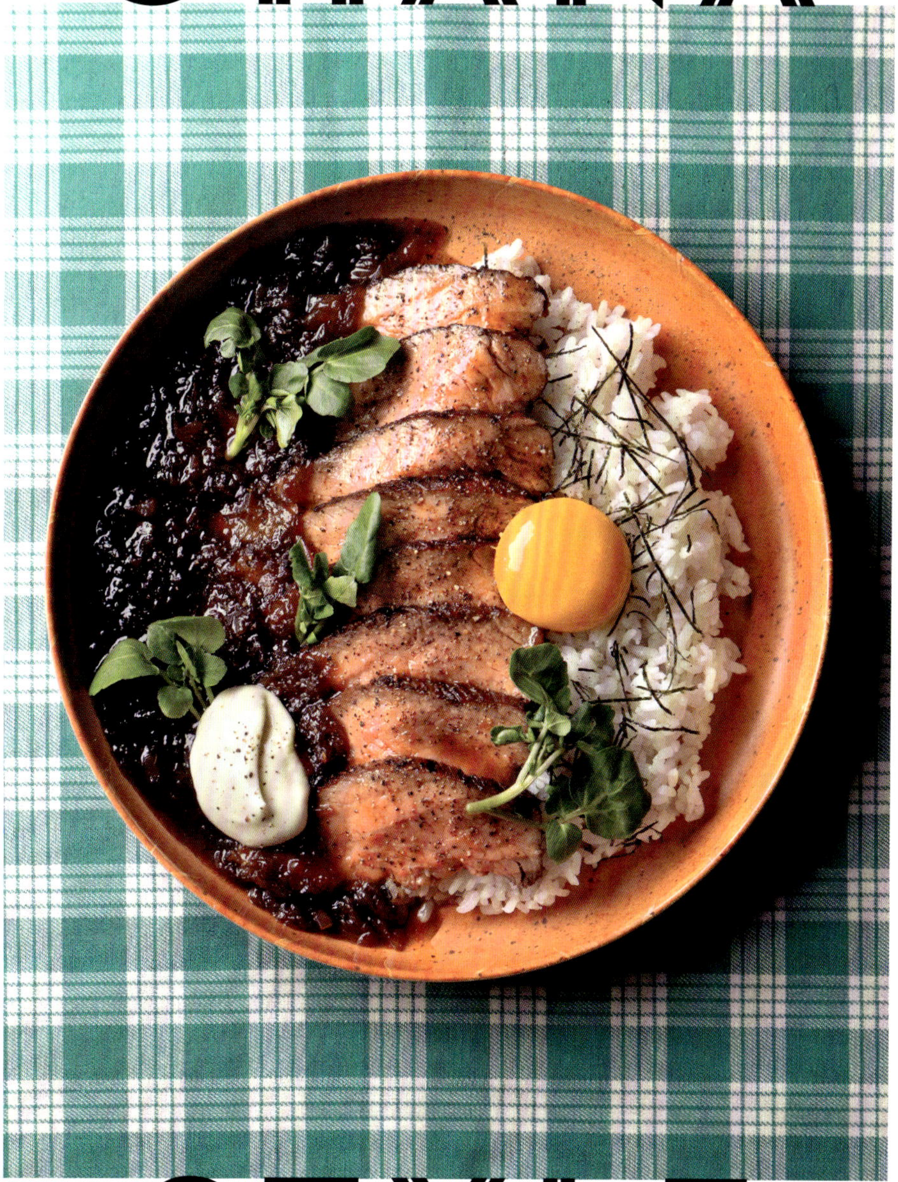

STYLE

WITH GARRETT SNYDER

PHOTOGRAPHS BY KEVIN MIYAZAKI

Pupus

Breakfast

Salads & Veggies

Noodles & Rice

T

Soups & Stews

Chicken & Seafood

Pork & Beef

Sauces & Pickles

Desserts & Drinks

My daughter Peyton with Auntie Merlie, who helped us care for Peyton when she was little and my wife and I were both working. It created a special bond between them.

Papa Rei and granddaughter Madison making Papa Rei's Tuna Patties

Mama's in the kitchen cooking dinner real nice
Beef stew on the stove, lomi salmon with the ice
We eat and drink and we sing all day
Kanikapila in the old Hawaiian way

—John Cruz, "Island Style"

Intro

The Hawaiian word *ohana* has many layers of meaning. On the most basic and literal level—as anyone who has watched *Lilo & Stitch* can tell you—it means family, as in the people who are related to you by blood. But it also refers to the larger social circles in your life: friends, friends of friends, neighbors, people you went to school with, elders whom you refer to as "auntie" and "uncle" even when they're not related to you. Zoom out beyond that, and on an even more abstract level, *ohana* means the people who provide you with a sense of belonging, and to whom, in turn, you feel an obligation and a responsibility. It was that last definition that stuck with me most when I asked myself when writing this book—what does it mean to cook for your ohana?

Writing a second cookbook is a lot like having a second kid. And by that I mean there's almost certainly a moment immediately after the first where you swear that you're never going through the process ever again, a feeling that almost certainly fades aways before you realize it. Now, although I have four kids, I can assure you that I currently do not plan on writing four cookbooks (much to my editor's relief). But I do think it's worth explaining where the kernel of an idea for this cookbook sprouted from.

The first was the reception for my first cookbook, *Cook Real Hawai'i*. Although I had spent nearly my whole life cooking local food, working on that project was the first moment I had to think deeply about what it all meant to me, and to see the bigger picture about how the many food traditions, history, and cultures of the islands fit together like a big colorful mosaic in the middle of the ocean. And I was honored that many people in my life seemed to have the same reaction to reading it, too—sometimes what's special about the things we grow up with aren't obvious to our own eyes, and it takes another way of documenting them to reveal what makes them exceptional.

The second was the pandemic. After working for decades in a restaurant kitchen, the majority of my time was spent cooking for others, which also meant it was only on my rare days off when I had the chance to cook for my own family—my wife, Janice, and our kids, Chloe, Peyton, Quinn, and Asher. When restaurants shut down in 2020, though, all that was flipped on its head. You could find me at home cooking breakfast, lunch, and dinner every day—and not just snacky meals, but full-on spreads of dishes. It even got to the point that Janice asked, Can we just have a snack? Something we can eat on the couch?

At the same time, I was also thinking about my restaurant ohana—the cooks, cashiers, and other people whom we employed at Tin Roof. We spent many months staying busy by cooking big family-style meals like pastele stew or chicken adobo and packaging them up for people in the community who were out of work or weren't able to cook for themselves.

What started to happen over time was that the lines between two worlds that were previously distinct started to blur and bleed together—cooking at the restaurant versus cooking at home, or cooking as a professional chef versus cooking for friends and family—until it changed the way I thought about cooking altogether.

These days I like to use the phrase "small kine homemade," which is a pidgin riff on the idea behind the old Sandra Lee cooking show *Semi-Homemade,* which was a favorite of mine on Food Network when I was just getting into cooking after high school. If you're not familiar with it, the concept of the show was using different techniques to combine store-bought items with fresh ingredients to make food that was fun and delicious. This was far from a foreign idea to me. My dad, Renoir Simeon—aka Papa Rei to his grandkids—was the king of cooking dishes with a "use what get" mentality. He never thought less of a recipe or dish because it used something that came from a can, as evidenced by his famous pan-fried tuna patties (page 42). *The main thing, the buggah is ONO!* as he would say: What matters is that it's delicious.

The other side of this mentality, however, is that paying attention to small, simple details—and knowing which ones are important enough to fuss over—can make all the difference in making a meal feel special. When I was growing up, it was very common for us to have guests over during family dinner. Aunts, uncles, and cousins just dropped in to hang out, or my dad's friends came over for pau hana beer and pupus. But even on a normal night, prior to when my mom fell ill, we would all sit down for a proper full meal. My mother would cook, my brother Jeremy and I would set the dining table full-on, with utensils sitting in their correct place next to folded napkins and cups of ice water. I was in charge of putting hot pads down on the table, and you best believe that if I didn't lay them out before my brother carried the pot of burning hot beef stew down from the stove, I would hear about it from him—*you f—n dummy!* We also made sure that the right condiments and accoutrements were on the table for whatever we were eating: shoyu for sashimi, Tabasco for stew, sliced tomato for adobo.

Nowadays, I'd be lying if I said that my own household operates with the same level of detail and steadfastness. Between running the restaurants and picking up the kids from school, cheerleading practices, and the like, life is so busy, busy, busy, it's a rare occasion when Janice or I have the time to prepare a proper meal. But when those occasions do come around, it's that special little half-twist, or attention to detail, that makes the memory. So if my friend Isaac suddenly gifts me some mahimahi fillets he snapped up on a fishing trip, I know they can be a fantastic dinner when I fry them in a pan and then make a quick pan sauce with lemon, capers, and cream (see Lemon Caper Mahi, page 176). If Chloe gets home from work and Peyton from cheer practice and everyone is starving, and all that's left in the freezer is some frozen dumplings, it doesn't take more than adding the leftover kimchi and shredded cheese in the fridge to impress them with some Loaded Mandoo (page 33).

When putting together the recipes for this book, my goal was for anyone—whether they are a kitchen pro or a novice—to be able to flip open to a random page and find something they can start cooking right away. Just dive in. That meant recipes that are simple but not simplistic, flexible, full of flavor, and, most of all, fun. Because why cook with ohana in the first place if not to bring happiness? I hope that as you make your way through this book, you'll find a recipe that speaks to every person in your life. There are the big gather-the-whole-crew dishes like Lechon Liempo (page 203)—a crispy-skinned pork belly roast—or a whole prime rib with soy sauce-infused jus (see page 223), or a sweet-savory umami-bomb Filipino Spaghetti Bake (page 107) that will entertain a crowd, but there are just as many everyone's-running-late breakfasts, the-cupboards-are-empty lunches, and something-from-nothing dinners—and don't worry, Janice, there are plenty of snacks, too. It's a sizable collection, but they all feature the same layered, complex mixture of Hawai'i flavor—a mix of Native Hawaiian, Filipino, Korean, Chinese, Japanese, and Portuguese influences and more—that have always defined what I cook, both at my restaurants and at home. And I hope they bring your ohana as much joy as they do mine.

There's another aspect to this book, and it has to do with the idea of legacy—what we share and pass on to our families when we cook together. As my coauthor Garrett and I were working on this, two very significant events took place in my life. The first was the opening of Tiffany's in our hometown of Wailuku on Maui. The original Tiffany's was what I would call a "no-frills" neighborhood bar and grill in the heart of Wailuku that had opened in the 2000s. Much like how we came to open Tin Roof, Tiffany's owners had decided to retire and wanted to sell the restaurant to someone local. As mom-and-pop business owners already, Janice and I knew how much work would be involved in starting a second spot, but we also realized how rare the opportunity was to have a restaurant a short drive down the road from our house that would act as a gathering place for the community. So, long story short, we went for it, and just like having a second kid (or writing a second cookbook), it was a decision that I'm prouder of every day. We're blessed with amazing local support and have become a destination for good food and drinks around Maui and beyond. Come see us.

At first, though, taking over Tiffany's wasn't easy. The people who had gone there for decades didn't want the menu or the prices to change. And on some level, I understood that. But I also knew that no business could survive solely on nostalgia, and that to serve classic local Hawai'i food the way I thought was important as a chef, I had to make it apparent why those changes were for the better. In other words, if you're going to mess with tradition, you'd better make sure it's an improvement. That same philosophy trickled down into the recipes in this book. Many of the dishes you'll find aren't traditional in the least. Some are evolutions, some are overhauls, and quite a few are just wild ideas that came from watching my daughter's TikTok feed that somehow worked out. But there was never one—even the salt 'n' pepper fish sticks—where I didn't ask myself, *What does this bring to the table over the original? And why does it need to exist?*

The other event that changed my life during this book was very different: the devastating wildfires in Lahaina in August 2023 that destroyed countless homes and businesses, cost a hundred people their lives, and changed Maui in ways that are still being felt even as we rebuild. Janice grew up on Maui's Westside, and we personally had many dear friends and relatives who lost everything in the fires, many who made the tough decision to relocate to the mainland due to the financial challenges of staying on Maui. This is sadly a common predicament for many born-and-raised families living in Hawaiʻi today—the islands are too expensive to stay, but too dear to leave. Among those who do end up relocating, sometimes there's a feeling that crops up: *If I no longer live in Hawaiʻi, am I still a local?* I hope this book answers that question with a resounding yes.

Just like the words *aloha* or *ohana* mean more than their literal definitions, I like to think that local food isn't confined to just Hawaiʻi as a place. It's transported everywhere in the traditions we share, the stories we tell, and the memories that stick around after. The one iconic dish that your family is famous for? Your version of tuna patties? You might prepare it a bit differently than your parents did, who almost certainly prepared it differently than *their* parents did. That's not a failure, that's transmission. So my wish is that if you encounter a recipe in this book that (hopefully) resonates with you on some level, it reminds you to look back at the traditions and memories of foods you grew up with in a fresh light. After all, cooking is just an excuse to connect with your ohana. And I hope this book provides you with plenty of excuses.

Mahalos,
Sheldon Simeon

PUPUS

Stir-Fried Olives

1 tablespoon neutral oil

2-inch piece fresh ginger, peeled and sliced

12 ounces high-quality olives, such as Castelvetrano, Kalamata, or a mix

4 cloves garlic, sliced

Zest of 1 large lemon, removed in wide strips

4 teaspoons oyster sauce

1 tablespoon extra-virgin olive oil

½ teaspoon freshly ground black pepper

SERVES 4 TO 6

Set a deep-sided 10-inch sauté pan or wok over medium-high heat, add the neutral oil, and heat until it just begins to smoke. Add the ginger and cook, stirring, until the slices are softened slightly, less than a minute. Add the olives, garlic, lemon zest, oyster sauce, olive oil, and pepper. Toss to coat. Cook, stirring or tossing often, until the olives are heated through, 3 to 4 minutes. Transfer to a bowl and let cool slightly before serving.

Some years back, I was a chef at a restaurant called Mala in Wailea, which was run by a talented chef named Mark Ellman. He had an appetizer on the menu that was called something like "warmed olives," basically cured olives heated gently in oil with garlic and other aromatics. But since the restaurant was extremely busy, the pans we used were almost never warm, but were, in fact, screaming hot from being in use all the time. That meant the warmed olives ended up more like stir-fried olives, which I always thought tasted better anyway. And I've been cooking them at home for parties that way ever since.

Aside from the usual seasonings that go well with olives—garlic, lemon, pepper, ginger—the MVP here is the slight wok hei flavor from the caramelized oyster sauce, which sizzles in the hot pan and turns into an umami-rich glaze that coats the olives and everything else with them in the pan. The salty olives are delicious, obviously, but I'd also highly recommend nibbling on the flash-fried garlic and sucking any residual flavor from the ginger slices and lemon peel as well.

Korean Cold Tofu

½ large seedless cucumber, thinly sliced

Kosher salt

4 teaspoons shoyu (soy sauce)

1 tablespoon toasted sesame oil

1 tablespoon sugar

1 large clove garlic, minced

2 teaspoons grated fresh ginger

3 scallions, thinly sliced

½ cup finely chopped kimchi, homemade (page 252) or store-bought

1 (14-ounce) package soft or medium-firm tofu, chilled, cut into ½-inch slices

¼ teaspoon toasted sesame seeds, for garnish

SERVES 2 OR 3

In a small bowl, toss the sliced cucumber with a few big pinches of salt and let sit for 5 minutes, or however long it takes to prepare the rest of the ingredients.

In another small bowl, whisk together the shoyu, sesame oil, sugar, garlic, and ginger until the sugar is dissolved. Stir in the scallions.

Rinse the salt off the cucumber, drain well, and return them to the same bowl. Combine with the chopped kimchi.

Arrange the tofu slices like fanned-out playing cards on a small plate, shallow bowl, or in a plastic container. Spread the cucumber/kimchi mixture evenly over the top, then spoon over the sesame-ginger dressing.

This dish can be eaten immediately, but it will taste just as good chilled in the fridge for up to a day or two. Sprinkle with sesame seeds before serving.

The cold tofu pupu was a fixture in our house when I was growing up. Grab a plate, plop down a package of tofu, top it with grated ginger and shoyu, and *boom*—instant snack. Tofu is the ultimate blank canvas and an ideal sponge for bold flavors (kid-me would treat cubes of tofu like literal sponges and double-dip in whatever bowl was in front of me).

Here, chilled tofu is taken to the next level with chopped kimchi, salted cucumbers, and seasonings that contrast with the mild soy milk flavor. Don't sweat not having everything on the ingredient list. The essentials are shoyu, sesame oil, and, of course, tofu. Beyond those, you're just enhancing and adding depth to the core dish (though you've probably got at least a little garlic and sugar hanging around, no?). Although you can use any type of tofu for this dish, I recommend soft or medium-firm tofu sold in the refrigerated section (rather than the kind that comes in shelf-stable packaging) for best flavor and texture.

"Smoked" Ahi Dip

8 ounces raw yellowfin tuna (see Note), cut into ½-inch chunks, or 2 (5-ounce) cans oil-packed tuna, well drained

½ cup diced sweet onion

3 tablespoons shoyu (soy sauce)

1 heaping teaspoon grated fresh ginger

1 teaspoon minced garlic

1 teaspoon toasted sesame oil

2 tablespoons neutral oil

8 ounces cream cheese, at room temperature

2 tablespoons sour cream

2 tablespoons mayonnaise

For serving

1 tablespoon neutral oil

2 tablespoons capers, drained

2 tablespoons thinly sliced scallions

Extra-virgin olive oil, for drizzling

Freshly ground black pepper

Lemon wedges, for squeezing

Club crackers, chips, or sliced baguette

SERVES 4

In a medium bowl, mix together the tuna, sweet onion, shoyu, ginger, garlic, and sesame oil. Marinate for 10 to 15 minutes.

Heat a large skillet over high heat. Add the neutral oil and swirl to coat the pan. Once the oil begins to smoke, add the marinated tuna and stir-fry until the tuna is fully cooked through, starts to flake, and is well charred around the edges (this is what provides the smoky flavor), 3 to 4 minutes. Remove the pan from the heat and transfer the tuna mixture to a large bowl.

Use a fork to break up any large chunks of tuna, then stir in the cream cheese, sour cream, and mayo until combined. Cover and place in the fridge to chill, ideally at least 1 hour (or as long as overnight) before serving.

When ready to serve: Line a plate with paper towels and have it near the stove. In a skillet over medium-high heat (the same one used to cook the tuna if you like), drizzle in the neutral oil and heat until shimmering. Add the capers and fry, stirring often, until browned and crispy, 4 to 5 minutes. Transfer the capers to the paper towels and let cool, then roughly chop.

To serve, spread the ahi dip onto a plate or shallow bowl, then top with the fried capers, scallions, a healthy drizzle of olive oil, and a big pinch of black pepper. Serve with lemon wedges and crackers on the side.

As essential to a trip to the beach as towels and slippers, smoked ahi dip is a classic tailgate snack of Hawai'i. Everyone's auntie has a recipe that their family swears by, even if they end up buying a quart container from the Foodland deli in a pinch.

The base isn't too different from other classic chip dips—there's cream cheese *and* sour cream, for one—but as you might guess, it's the smoked fish that makes it sparkle. Even then, I would argue the "smoked" element is negotiable. Many of my friends share the suspicion that one of the top-selling ahi dip brands on Maui (which shall go unnamed) is made with nothing more than basic canned tuna and some liquid smoke.

I am staunchly anti-liquid smoke, however. So when we put ahi dip on the menu at Tiffany's, the cooks and I came up with a workaround: searing shoyu-marinated tuna in a hot wok or pan, which replicates the smoky flavor through the sizzled shoyu. No smoker needed.

Note: Using fresh tuna is worth the effort here, but if you're going the canned route, look for high-quality solid tuna packed in oil rather than water.

Garlic Furikake Fries

For the garlic butter

3 tablespoons unsalted butter, melted

2 tablespoons minced garlic

1 tablespoon finely chopped fresh parsley

For the fries

2 pounds russet potatoes (3 to 4 potatoes) or frozen fries

Peanut oil or other neutral oil, for frying

2 tablespoons cornstarch

Kosher salt and freshly ground black pepper

For serving

Freshly grated Parmesan cheese

Furikake (see Note)

Mustard-Mayo Fry Sauce (page 258), for serving

SERVES 6

Make the garlic butter: In a small bowl, stir together the melted butter, garlic, and parsley. Set aside at room temperature.

Frozen-Fry Method

Preheat the oven to the temperature listed on the frozen fries packaging (usually 450°F). Line a large baking sheet with parchment paper.

Arrange the frozen fries in a single layer. Bake as directed until crispy and golden brown.

Oven-Fry Method

Preheat the oven to 450°F. Line a large baking sheet with parchment paper.

Peel and wash the potatoes, then cut them into long ¼-inch-thick strips resembling fries.

Place the potatoes in a large microwave-safe bowl and cover tightly with plastic wrap. Microwave on high for 4 minutes to "blanch" the potatoes with steam before they go into the oven. Let the potatoes cool slightly before removing the plastic wrap, as steam can escape and cause burns. Place on a bed of paper towels or a wire rack to cool further and dry off any remaining moisture.

In a small bowl, whisk together ¼ cup peanut oil, the cornstarch, and a few big pinches of salt and pepper. In a large bowl or sealable plastic bag, combine the potatoes and the oil mixture, tossing well to coat.

When I lived on O'ahu, I used to go watch volleyball matches at the University of Hawai'i—I had some friends on the team from when I'd played in high school. The strongest memories from those games weren't the spikes and serves, but the garlic fries I would get at the concession booth. Garlic fries are a popular stadium food in Hawai'i, and usually you can smell them from the parking lot. It's a shame more people don't make them at home, at least that I know of, but I'm doing my part to change that (and make the process a bit easier, too).

I make my fries one of three ways. The first is the easiest: packaged frozen fries. The second, which has the highest effort-to-quality ratio, is steaming the potatoes slightly in the microwave, then tossing them with oil and baking them until crispy. The third is the same way I make fries at the restaurant: parboiling the potatoes, then deep-frying them twice in peanut oil at two temperatures, which produces those perfect ultimate crispy-outside, fluffy-inside fries. Since the seasoning goes on after cooking, any of these methods can work for these fully loaded garlic fries coated with butter, Parmesan, and sweet-salty furikake. Take care that you're tossing the potatoes immediately after cooking, as that's the key to getting everything to stick.

Arrange the potatoes in a single layer on the lined baking sheet. Bake until the potatoes are crispy and golden brown, 25 to 30 minutes, stirring after 15 minutes. Sprinkle the fries with a pinch more salt and pepper after removing them from the oven.

Double-Fry Method

Peel and wash the potatoes, then cut them into long ¼-inch-thick strips resembling fries. Soak the potato strips in cold water for about 30 minutes (or as long as overnight).

Drain the water and rinse the potatoes two or three times, shaking off any water to get rid of the excess starch.

Fill a large pot with water and bring to a boil. Add the potatoes and cook for 5 to 6 minutes, just until they can be pierced by a fork—you don't want them to be so soft that they break. Drain well and let cool slightly, then arrange the fries on a large sheet pan.

Use a few paper towels to pat the fries as dry as possible and sprinkle them with the cornstarch, shaking the pan and flipping the fries so each one is coated evenly.

Line a baking sheet with paper towels, set a rack over the paper towels, and have it near the stove. Pour 2 inches of peanut oil into a 5- to 6-quart Dutch oven or deep pot and heat over medium-low heat until the oil reads 250°F on a deep-fry thermometer.

Working in batches of two handfuls at a time so the pot doesn't get overcrowded, add the potatoes to the hot oil and cook, stirring occasionally, until light brown, 5 to 7 minutes. They won't be crispy, but they should hold their shape well. Transfer to the wire rack to drain any excess oil.

Once the potatoes have all been parcooked, increase the heat to medium and wait until the oil reaches 350°F. Working in batches again, add the fries back to the oil and fry, making sure to move them around so they evenly brown and crisp up, until a deep golden color, 3 to 4 minutes. Transfer the fries to the wire rack to drain, then sprinkle with salt and pepper.

For serving (all methods): Transfer the hot fries to a large bowl. While tossing or stirring with one hand, drizzle on the reserved garlic butter, then sprinkle on as much Parmesan and furikake as you like. Once the fries are coated evenly, serve immediately with mustard-mayo sauce for dipping.

Note: I'm using a basic store-bought variety of furikake called nori fumi, which can be found in many supermarkets and contains just nori, sesame seeds, sugar, and salt. Don't worry if the furikake you have doesn't have the same exact name, as long as it has close to that combination of seasonings.

Shrimp Cocktail Tostadas

2 pounds tail-on jumbo shrimp, peeled and deveined, and thawed if frozen (see Notes)

½ teaspoon baking soda

Kosher salt

1 medium red onion, diced

¼ cup fresh lime juice

½ cup fresh orange juice, plus more to taste

1 large seedless cucumber, diced

½ cup ketchup

1 large jalapeño, seeded and finely chopped

3 tablespoons finely chopped fresh cilantro, leaves and stems

2 tablespoons tomato paste

1 tablespoon Worcestershire sauce

1 tablespoon prepared horseradish, drained

1 teaspoon ground cumin

½ teaspoon garlic powder

Freshly ground black pepper

In a large bowl, toss the shrimp with the baking soda and 1 teaspoon salt. Cover with plastic wrap and place in the fridge to chill for 15 minutes.

In another large bowl, combine the red onion and lime juice and set aside.

Fill a large pot with 2 quarts of water and bring to a boil. Once boiling, reduce the heat to a simmer and stir in 2 tablespoons salt and the orange juice. Add the shrimp and simmer until they turn pink and are cooked all the way through, 3 to 4 minutes.

Drain the shrimp carefully, rinse under cold running water until they are no longer warm, then drain well again. Remove the tails and cut the shrimp into ½-inch pieces.

recipe and ingredients continue →

I've always been a shrimp head. If you ever see me walk into an all-you-can-eat buffet and they have a platter on ice, no doubt that will be filling up my first plate. I think my fascination dates back to when I was fresh out of culinary school and left Hawaiʻi for the first time to work at Disney World. At some point, I was promoted to fry cook at the now-defunct Living Seas at Epcot restaurant, which did these retro shrimp cocktails in glass sundae bowls. They were popular, so the restaurant's walk-in fridge was filled with hundreds of racks of boiled jumbo shrimp—like Scrooge McDuck's vault of gold except it was shellfish. Sometimes I would sneak in there, eat a few, then fill my pockets with a few dozen more and snack on them like popcorn during the rest of my shift.

Despite all the shrimp I've crushed, I always have a tough time settling on a favorite preparation. I love a dead simple American-shrimp cocktail with ketchupy sauce and lots of horseradish, and I also love Mexican-style coctel de camaron with savory, tomatoey broth and chopped cucumbers and avocado. This recipe is a happy marriage of the two. Start by investing in good-quality shrimp (see Notes), preferably with the tail on to add flavor during cooking. Then briefly cure them with baking soda, which helps maintain that snappy, bouncy texture once they're cooked, and add a glug of orange juice to the poaching broth to neutralize any potential residual baking soda bitterness (Chemistry 101: acid neutralizes base). Assemble the cocktail, chill for an hour, and shrimp heaven on a tostada awaits.

Notes: My definition of high-quality shrimp usually means wild-caught shrimp sourced from the US or Mexico (Argentinian wild shrimp are great, too), ideally sized at least 21/25 shrimp per pound (jumbo grade) or larger.

Frozen is often a better bet than fresh due to its consistency and wider availability, but just make sure the shrimp are fully thawed before cooking, which can be done quickly by running them under cold water.

For serving

1 large avocado

Mayonnaise

Tostadas

Mexican hot sauce, such as Tapatío

Cilantro leaves or microgreens (optional), for garnish

SERVES 4 TO 6

Add the shrimp to the bowl with the onion and lime juice, along with the cucumber, ketchup, jalapeño, cilantro, tomato paste, Worcestershire, horseradish, cumin, and garlic powder, tossing to combine. Depending on how soupy you prefer your shrimp cocktail, drizzle in a little orange juice until you reach your desired consistency. Taste and season with salt and pepper. Chill at least 1 hour before serving or, if you don't plan on eating immediately, cover and store in the fridge for up to a day.

When ready to serve, peel the avocado and dice it into ½-inch chunks. Carefully fold the avocado into the shrimp. Spread a thin layer of mayo on the tostadas and top with the shrimp cocktail and a few shakes of hot sauce and a few sprigs of cilantro or other greens, if on hand.

Justin Cantere, once a cook in my kitchens, who is now forging his own path as a culinary entrepreneur and Maui fisherman, with his wife, Shekinah, and their kids

Sticky Fish Sauce Wings

For the sauce

2 cups apple cider vinegar

2 cups sugar

1 cup fish sauce

4 tablespoons minced garlic

2 tablespoons chili garlic sauce or sambal oelek

For the wings

2 pounds whole chicken wings, thawed if frozen (can also substitute with drumettes and flats)

½ cup whole milk

1 teaspoon kosher salt, plus more to taste

½ teaspoon freshly ground black pepper, plus more to taste

3 tablespoons minced garlic

1 cup all-purpose flour

1 cup cornstarch

1 teaspoon garlic powder

½ teaspoon baking soda

Neutral oil, for frying

For serving

¼ cup finely chopped mint or cilantro (or a mixture of the two)

¼ cup fried garlic, homemade (recipe follows) or store-bought

¼ cup finely crushed honey-roasted peanuts

Lime wedges

SERVES 4 TO 6

Make the sauce: In a small saucepan, stir together the vinegar and sugar. Bring the mixture to a boil over medium heat, reduce the heat, and simmer, stirring occasionally, until the mixture is reduced by one-third, about 10 minutes. Transfer the sauce to a heatproof jar and stir in the fish sauce, minced garlic, and chili garlic sauce. Blend with an immersion blender until smooth (this step is optional for a smoother glaze). Set aside.

Prepare the wings: In a large bowl or resealable plastic bag, add the chicken wings, milk, salt, black pepper, and minced garlic. Mix well and let marinate for at least 30 minutes at room temperature, or up to 2 hours in the fridge.

In a medium bowl, stir together the all-purpose flour, cornstarch, garlic powder, baking soda, plus a generous pinch of salt and black pepper. Scoop out ½ cup of the flour mixture into another small bowl, then whisk with ⅔ cup water to form a thin batter. Remove the wings from the marinade and pat them dry with paper towels, then discard the marinade.

When you're ready to fry, set up a dredging station with the two bowls and the chicken wings arranged next to the pot in which you're frying.

Line a baking sheet with paper towels and have it near the stove. Pour 2 inches of oil into a large pot or Dutch oven deep enough for frying and heat over medium-high heat until it reaches 350°F. (You can also add a drop of batter to test. If it instantly sizzles but doesn't burn immediately, you're at temp.)

recipe continues →

We serve these Vietnamese-inspired wings as a late-night special at Tiffany's from time to time because they're the kind of fried drinking snack every neighborhood bar should serve: sweet and tangy with crackly skin and a sauce that clings to your fingers. Even with all the different flavors and textures happening, it's as easy to put together at home as any fried wing recipe. A combination of vinegar, fish sauce, and sugar is the foundation for the incredible sticky glaze. Soaking the chicken wings in milk (a mild acid) before frying will help tenderize the meat without making it mushy. Finish them with a coating of chopped herbs and something crunchy—here I'm using cilantro, crushed peanuts, and fried garlic, but you can also use things like basil, fried onions, or sunflower seeds.

Working in batches of 4 to 5 wings, dip each wing into the batter, letting the excess drip off, then coat thoroughly in the flour mixture, shaking off any extra flour. Add to the oil and fry the wings until golden brown, turning every couple of minutes, until they're cooked through, 8 to 10 minutes. (Tip: Check the first wing for any pink or red meat near the bone and increase the cooking time if needed.) Drain the wings on the paper towels. In a large bowl, toss the wings with the sticky fish sauce.

To serve: Garnish the wings with the herbs, fried garlic, and crushed peanuts. Squeeze the lime wedges on top.

Fried Garlic MAKES ABOUT ¼ CUP

⅓ cup minced garlic (about 16 cloves)

Neutral oil

Kosher salt

Sugar

Place the garlic in a medium microwave-safe bowl and add enough oil to cover (at least 3 tablespoons). Microwave for 1 minute, then stir. Repeat, stirring and microwaving in 30-second increments until the garlic begins to brown. Then repeat, stirring and microwaving in 15-second increments, until the garlic is a deep golden color. (This could take between 2 and 4 minutes total, depending on your microwave.)

Set a sieve over a bowl and pour in the garlic and oil. Reserve the oil for various garlic oil uses (it can be stored at room temp for up to 1 week). Transfer the garlic to a plate lined with paper towels and season with a pinch each of salt and sugar. Set aside to cool before using.

Loaded Mandoo

- Neutral oil, for frying
- ½ medium yellow onion, thinly sliced
- ½ cup roughly chopped kimchi, with juices
- 1 teaspoon shoyu (soy sauce) or pinch of kosher salt
- 12 frozen dumplings (mandoo, gyoza, or similar)
- ½ cup shredded mozzarella cheese
- ¼ cup mayonnaise
- 1 tablespoon sriracha or 2 teaspoons gochujang (Korean chile paste)
- 1 clove garlic, grated
- ½ teaspoon toasted sesame oil
- 1 medium Roma tomato, seeded and diced
- Handful of chopped fresh cilantro
- Handful of chopped scallions
- Chili oil (optional), for serving

SERVES 2

In a large skillet or nonstick pan with a lid, heat 1 tablespoon neutral oil over medium heat until it shimmers. Add the onion, kimchi, and shoyu and cook, stirring often, until the onion has softened, the juices of the kimchi have evaporated, and the mixture begins to caramelize, 3 to 4 minutes. Transfer the kimchi-onion mixture to a small bowl, give the pan a quick wipe with a paper towel, and return the pan to medium heat.

Drizzle in 2 tablespoons neutral oil (or slightly more if your pan isn't nonstick), then arrange the dumplings, flat-side down, in a tight row or circle so they're shoulder to shoulder. Cook until browned on the bottoms, 2 to 3 minutes.

Add enough water to just cover the bottom of the pan (about ⅓ cup for a 12-inch pan), cover, and cook until the water has evaporated and the dumpling skins have softened, another 2 to 3 minutes.

Uncover and carefully spoon the kimchi-onion mixture evenly over the dumplings, then sprinkle the mozzarella on top before replacing the lid. Continue to cook for about another minute, until the cheese melts. Remove the pan from heat and let sit, covered, while you prepare the sauce.

In a small bowl, whisk together the mayo, sriracha, garlic, and sesame oil until combined, adding a little water as needed until it reaches a drizzle-able consistency.

To serve, carefully lift or slide the dumpling raft (held together by molten cheese) onto a plate and top with the chopped tomato, cilantro, and scallions. Drizzle with as much spicy mayo and chili oil (if using) as desired.

Once my kids became old enough to use a stove—in our family that's around age six, still supervised, of course—they were automatically enrolled in the first three courses of Simeon cooking school. The first is learning to cook eggs (scrambled, then fried), the second is making ramen (the instant kind), and the third (and best lesson) is cooking potstickers, also known as mandoo, or gyoza, or what have you. It's a straightforward process, but one that requires visual feedback and timing, two crucial skills for pint-size cooks. Also, without a doubt, there has not been a moment in the past decade when my house has not had at least one, often multiple, bulk bags of potstickers in the freezer. Quinn, who's now fourteen, is the official dumpling deputy of our house, and can always be relied upon to cook a batch when the rest of us need a last-minute meal, which is pretty much weekly it seems like.

Even the greatest frozen potstickers can get a little boring, though, which is where this dish comes in handy. It's the dumpling equivalent of loaded nachos or potato skins, made in the pan you're already using to cook the potstickers. The sautéed onion-kimchi is a base layer for the gooey, molten mozzarella, which gets finished with chopped tomatoes, scallions, and spicy mayo.

Croissant Toasts
with Hot Honey Tomatoes & Whipped Ricotta

1 pint cherry tomatoes

3 cloves garlic, minced

⅓ cup plus 2 teaspoons extra-virgin olive oil

4 plain croissants

Softened salted butter

3 tablespoons apple cider vinegar

2 tablespoons honey

2 teaspoons chili garlic sauce or sambal oelek

1 teaspoon shoyu (soy sauce)

Kosher salt and freshly ground black pepper

1 cup whole-milk ricotta cheese

Grated zest of 1 lemon

2 teaspoons fresh lemon juice

¼ cup chopped fresh herbs (any combination of mint, dill, or basil)

SERVES 4

Preheat the oven to 400°F.

Arrange the tomatoes and garlic on a 9 × 13-inch baking sheet or a similar-size baking pan and drizzle with ⅓ cup of the olive oil. Roast undisturbed, until the tomatoes are blistered and soft, 15 to 20 minutes. Remove from the oven and let cool.

While the tomatoes are roasting, place a large skillet over medium heat. Using a rolling pin, flatten each croissant until they're as thin as you can get them, then spread a thin layer of butter on each side. Working in batches, toast the flat croissants in the skillet until browned and crispy, about 3 minutes per side, pressing them down to develop a nice crust. Remove them from the pan and let cool.

In a medium bowl, whisk together the vinegar, honey, chili garlic sauce, and shoyu. Gently fold in the roasted tomatoes and any oil remaining in the pan. Season with salt and pepper to taste.

In a small bowl, combine the ricotta, the remaining 2 teaspoons olive oil, the lemon zest, and lemon juice. Blend with an immersion blend or electric mixer on low speed until the ricotta is light and fluffy, about 2 minutes. Season with salt and pepper to taste.

To serve, spread each croissant with a layer of whipped ricotta. Spoon the tomato salad on top and garnish with the chopped herbs. Serve immediately.

Have you ever bought one of those giant containers of croissants at Costco and not been able to finish it? Happens all the time in our family. Everyone loves fresh croissants, nobody loves day-old croissants. That is until I realized that leftover croissants are essentially prebuttered toast, and they turn out great when you squish them down and griddle them in a hot pan until they're flaky and crispy once more (look at the "flat croissant" trend on TikTok to see what I mean). Here, I'm pairing some crispy croissant toasts with a low-effort combination that would be just as good over any type of toasted bread: jammy roasted tomatoes in a sweet-spicy honey vinegar sauce with fluffy whipped ricotta. Great for impressing any friends invited over for brunch—no mention of leftover croissants necessary.

Pimento Cheese Mochi Bread

- 2½ cups mochiko flour (glutinous rice flour)
- 1½ cups freshly grated extra-sharp Cheddar cheese
- 1 (4-ounce) jar or can diced pimentos, drained
- ¼ cup freshly grated Parmesan cheese
- 1½ teaspoons kosher salt
- 1 teaspoon garlic powder
- 1 teaspoon onion powder
- ½ teaspoon freshly ground black pepper
- 1 cup buttermilk
- 2 large eggs, lightly beaten
- ½ cup mayonnaise
- 1 tablespoon yellow mustard
- 2 teaspoons Worcestershire sauce
- 1 teaspoon Tabasco hot sauce
- Melted salted butter, for brushing

MAKES ABOUT 36 PIECES

Preheat the oven to 400°F. Line a baking sheet with parchment paper.

In a large bowl, stir together the mochiko flour, Cheddar, pimentos, Parmesan, salt, garlic powder, onion powder, and black pepper. In a medium bowl, whisk together the buttermilk, eggs, mayo, mustard, Worcestershire sauce, and Tabasco. Pour the buttermilk mixture into the flour a bit at a time, stirring and folding with a silicone spatula and/or kneading with your hands, until a sticky loose dough forms with no dry lumps. Don't worry about overmixing. (Or, if you have a stand mixer with a dough hook or paddle attachment, it can be used on low speed for this step as well.)

Using a spoon, drop rounded balls of dough the size of Ping-Pong balls onto the lined baking sheet at least 1 inch apart and brush with melted butter.

Bake until the tops are lightly browned, 15 to 20 minutes.

Serve warm. Any leftovers can be covered and stored in the fridge for up to 1 week, and reheated by microwaving for 10 to 15 seconds, until warm, or baking in a 350°F oven or toaster oven for a few minutes.

What's better than pimento cheese? Pimento cheese in mochi form. Think of this as a Hawai'i-Filipino version of the Brazilian cheese balls pão de queijo, made with mochi flour instead of cassava flour. And while pimento cheese has a strong association with the South in the United States, it's just as popular in the Philippines. Although you'll sometimes see mochiko flour labeled as glutinous rice flour, it actually contains no gluten, which makes this party-friendly recipe ideal for those who are gluten-sensitive.

Last-Minute Spinach Rolls

2 (10-ounce) boxes frozen chopped spinach, thawed and squeezed dry

1 cup mayonnaise

1 cup sour cream

½ cup chopped cooked bacon (from about 6 slices)

3 scallions, finely chopped

1 (1-ounce) package ranch dressing mix, vegetable soup mix, or green onion dip mix

¼ teaspoon freshly ground black pepper

8 burrito-size (10-inch) flour tortillas

SERVES 8

In a large bowl, combine the squeezed spinach, mayo, sour cream, bacon, scallions, seasoning mix, and pepper. Spread the mixture evenly edge-to-edge onto each tortilla using an offset spatula, then roll them up sushi-style. Cover and refrigerate until ready to serve (they can be made the night before).

Slice into 2-inch-thick rounds (or whatever size is desired) before serving.

We've all been there: You were supposed to make a dish for a party that you forgot about, or it slipped your mind that you're on the hook for snack at your kid's school this week. That's why spinach rolls exist. These are an iconic staple of local gatherings that date back to the era of seventies *Good Housekeeping* "easy recipe" booklets. Whenever they show up on the potluck line, there's a good chance whoever made them pulled off an eleventh-hour miracle. No one minds, though, because spinach dip pinwheels are true crowd-pleasers. While it's important to invest in real chopped bacon rather than bacon-flavored "bits," using frozen spinach is counterintuitively better than fresh spinach, as it's more tender and easily mixable. Be sure to firmly squeeze out as much liquid from the thawed greens as possible so you don't dilute the creamy spread.

Shoyu Hot Dogs

- 1 (12-ounce) package hot dogs
- 2 teaspoons neutral oil
- ½ cup thinly sliced sweet onion
- ¼ cup shoyu (soy sauce)
- ¼ cup light brown sugar
- Freshly ground black pepper
- Cooked white rice (optional), for serving

SERVES 2 TO 4

To make the octopus hot dogs (see Note), cut each hot dog in half crosswise (the rounded ends of the hot dog will be the octopus heads). From the cut side, carefully split the hot dog halves lengthwise, leaving the last inch or so unsplit (i.e., don't split the hot dog half all the way through). Split the half-dog once more to create 4 tentacles. You might end up with a severed octopus leg here or there, but don't worry.

In a medium skillet, heat the oil over medium-high heat until shimmering. Add the hot dog octopi to the pan and cook, stirring frequently but gently, until they start to brown at the edges and the legs curl up, 3 to 4 minutes. Transfer the dogs to a plate while you make the sauce.

Add the onions to the hot pan and cook just until they become fragrant, less than a minute. Add ¼ cup water, followed by the shoyu and brown sugar. Stir until the sugar is dissolved.

Continue cooking until the sauce starts to thicken, 3 to 4 minutes. Return the hot dogs to the pan, tossing them gently to coat in the sauce. Season with a pinch of pepper. Remove from the heat and serve as a pupu or over rice (if using), with any remaining sauce drizzled on top.

Shoyu wieners hold a special place in my heart. My dad would cook these all the time for me growing up, and I loved them, but then at some point into adulthood I completely forgot about them. Until I had kids. Then one day my dad cooked my kids some, and the memories rushed back. He even busted out the famed hot dog octopus technique. Shoyu hot dogs are the pinnacle of small-kid food and a standby when supplies are low. Throw in some onion if get, but all that's really required is shoyu and sugar to make the hot dog glaze. I like to use all-beef dogs, but whatever is on sale will work, too. Serve with rice and baby carrots and you've got near-instant toddler lunch.

Note: For an easier but less kid-thrilling version, simply slice the hot dog into ½-inch coins on the diagonal and leave them in the pan while you make the shoyu glaze.

Papa Rei's Tuna Patties

1 (10.5-ounce) can cream of mushroom soup

2 (5-ounce) cans tuna packed in oil, drained

1 large egg

1 (7.75-ounce) bag sour cream & onion potato chips, crushed

1 cup panko bread crumbs

Neutral oil, for frying

MAKES 10 PATTIES

In a medium bowl, mix the cream of mushroom soup, drained tuna, and egg until combined. Stir in the crushed potato chips. Cover and chill in the fridge for 15 to 20 minutes, until the mixture firms up slightly.

Spread out the panko in a shallow dish. Use your hands to shape the chilled tuna mixture into 10 patties about ½ inch thick. Evenly coat both sides of each patty with the panko.

Line a baking sheet with paper towels and have it near the stove. In a large skillet, heat enough oil to generously coat the bottom of the pan over medium heat until shimmering. Place half the patties in the skillet. Use a spatula to gently flatten the patties to make sure they get even contact with the pan. Cook until golden brown and crispy on both sides, about 3 minutes per side. Drain the cooked patties on the paper towels. Cook the remaining patties and serve warm.

Other than the Pork & Peas from my first cookbook, this is the most requested Simeon family recipe. People would ask Pops to cook this at any and all family events. And I'll be the first to admit, it's an unusual one. In fact, the reason these pan-fried tuna patties didn't go in the first cookbook was that they were so common to us, they didn't even register to me as a recipe to write down. But here we are. I'm not sure where this dish originated, but if it's Filipino, it isn't traditional. What I can tell you is that it's 100 percent undeniably, inexplicably *ono*. There's something about the combination of sour cream and onion potato chips and canned tuna (packed in oil, not the tasteless kind in water) that works on a fundamental level, like those casserole recipes that just don't taste the same without a can of condensed mushroom soup. This is also a great simple recipe for kids: Asher patted out a batch by hand with Papa Rei the other week. If you're somehow still skeptical, I'll add this: You probably have the ingredients in your cupboard already. Why not grab a frying pan and go make a snack?

BREAKFAST

Mango Sticky Rice Waffles
with Coconut Syrup

3 cups chilled leftover cooked short-grain rice

1 (13-ounce) can full-fat coconut milk

3 teaspoons cornstarch

1 teaspoon baking powder

1 tablespoon sugar

½ teaspoon kosher salt, plus more as needed

3 tablespoons maple syrup

1 teaspoon vanilla extract

1 tablespoon butter or margarine, plus more for greasing the waffle iron

2 ripe mangoes, sliced

SERVES 4

Place the rice in a microwave-safe medium bowl and microwave for 1 to 2 minutes, stirring once, until it's hot (not just warm) throughout.

Shake the can of coconut milk well before opening. Pour half the coconut milk over the rice, then add 1 teaspoon of the cornstarch, the baking powder, sugar, and salt. Stir until well combined and the warm rice has absorbed the coconut milk. Set aside.

In a small saucepan, combine the remaining coconut milk, the maple syrup, vanilla, and a pinch of salt and bring to a boil over medium heat. Meanwhile, in a small bowl, whisk together the remaining 2 teaspoons cornstarch with 2 teaspoons water until smooth to form a slurry. Once the coconut sauce starts to boil, reduce the heat to low and stir in the slurry. Continue stirring until the mixture has thickened, another 2 to 3 minutes. Remove from the heat and stir in the 1 tablespoon butter until melted. Keep warm.

Preheat the oven to 200°F, if you'd like, to keep the finished waffles warm.

Preheat a waffle iron, then brush liberally with butter or margarine. For a regular-size waffle maker, measure out 1 firmly packed cup of the rice mixture (try not to overload it) and cook until golden brown and crispy, 4 to 5 minutes. If you're using the oven to keep the waffles warm, transfer directly to the oven rack. Repeat until you have waffled all the sticky rice.

Serve the waffles topped with mango slices and the warm coconut syrup.

Any recipe that uses leftover rice in our house is more valuable than gold. And while fried rice will always be the greatest in that category, a breakfast-friendly version of mango sticky rice is a close second. I think the original idea for these waffles came from one of the kids seeing a viral video where someone made waffles from leftover holiday stuffing and fried rice and covered them in gravy. Sometime later, after we had ordered Thai takeout, I thought, *Hmm, I bet that coconut sticky rice would be very delicious if we stuck the leftovers in a waffle iron.* To no one's surprise, it was incredible.

Here I'm mixing cooked short-grain rice with cornstarch so that it mimics the consistency of sticky rice, then using it as a coconutty waffle batter that's dairy-free and gluten-free. Be patient and allow the waffle time to crisp and brown—the fat in the coconut milk and brush of butter or margarine on the waffle iron will prevent sticking, and once it reaches optimum crisping, it should release easily.

Banana Pancakes
with Chantilly Cream

For the Chantilly cream

4 ounces cream cheese, at room temperature

⅓ cup powdered sugar

¼ cup sour cream

1 teaspoon vanilla extract

1 cup heavy cream

For the pancakes

2 ripe bananas, cut into slices

1½ cups whole milk

3 tablespoons salted butter, melted, plus more for the griddle

2 large eggs, separated

½ cup chopped toasted pecans or walnuts (optional)

1½ cups all-purpose flour

2 tablespoons granulated sugar

2 teaspoons baking powder

½ teaspoon kosher salt

For serving

Salted butter, melted

Maple syrup

2 ripe bananas, sliced crosswise

Ground cinnamon

MAKES 12 PANCAKES

Make the Chantilly cream: In the bowl of a stand mixer fitted with the whisk (or in a medium bowl and using a hand mixer), combine the cream cheese, powdered sugar, sour cream, and vanilla. Mix well by hand. Pour in the heavy cream and whip on medium-high speed until stiff peaks form, 3 to 4 minutes. What you're looking for is a smooth but stiff whipped cream. If you like, transfer the cream to a resealable bag or piping bag for serving. Place in the fridge until ready to use, up to overnight.

Make the pancakes: In a large bowl, mash the sliced bananas well with a fork. Add the milk, melted butter, egg yolks (only the yolks), and the chopped nuts (if using). Whisk until combined. Add the flour, granulated sugar, baking powder, and salt and stir well with a spatula just until combined (it's okay if there are a few lumps).

In another medium bowl with an electric mixer, beat the egg whites on medium-high speed until stiff peaks form, about 2 minutes. Scrape the beaten egg whites into the batter using the spatula and gently fold to combine. Don't overmix.

Place a griddle or large nonstick skillet over medium-low heat and lightly brush with butter. Pour in ¼ cup of batter for each pancake, separating them by at least 1 inch. Cook until bubbles form on top and the bottom is lightly browned, about 3 minutes, adjusting the heat to prevent burning. Flip and continue cooking until golden on the other side, about another minute. Transfer to a plate. Repeat with the remaining batter, brushing the pan with butter as needed.

To serve: In a medium bowl or measuring cup, combine the melted butter and maple syrup in a 1-to-5 ratio (warm syrup in the microwave if you like). Plate a pancake, spread on a thick layer of Chantilly cream, top with a few slices of banana, then sprinkle lightly with cinnamon. Repeat with as many layers of pancake as desired. Serve drizzled with the butter-maple syrup.

Chantilly cream is thought to have originated in France at the Château de Chantilly. How it got from there to Hawai'i, I don't know, but Hawai'i bakeries go wild for the stuff—Chantilly cakes, Chantilly cream puffs, Chantilly everything. I think of it as the baby of whipped cream and pastry cream, but less finicky. In my version, sour cream adds tang and cream cheese adds texture.

As for the pancakes, if you're going to the trouble of making them from scratch, take the simple extra step of separating and beating your egg whites. These will be the fluffy, lightest banana pancakes you've ever eaten.

Finally, the syrup. Here's a secret of great brunch places: Use real maple syrup and always mix it with butter. Start with a 1-to-5 ratio of butter to syrup by volume (e.g., 1 tablespoon butter for ⅓ cup syrup) and adjust depending on your taste.

Black Sesame Sweet Rolls

For the rolls

Softened butter, for the pan

2 tablespoons brown sugar

½ cup Black Sesame Butter (page 254)

All-purpose flour, for dusting

1 (8-ounce) can crescent rolls (or crescent dough sheet)

2 tablespoons butter, at room temperature

For the frosting

2 ounces (¼ cup) cream cheese, at room temperature

2 tablespoons butter, at room temperature

½ cup powdered sugar

½ teaspoon kosher salt

2 teaspoons black sesame seeds

½ teaspoon toasted sesame oil

MAKES 6 ROLLS

Make the rolls: Preheat the oven to 375°F. Butter a 9 × 9-inch baking pan.

In a small bowl, mix the brown sugar and black sesame butter until combined, using a fork to break up any clumps.

If desired, lightly dust a working surface with flour to prevent the dough from sticking. Carefully unroll the crescent dough and spread out onto the work surface in one sheet, firmly pressing any perforations to seal if needed. Evenly spread the sesame butter mixture across the entire surface of the dough, edge to edge. Starting on a short side, roll the dough up into a log and pinch the seam closed. Cut the log into 6 rolls of equal width. Arrange the rolls in the greased baking pan.

Bake until the rolls are lightly browned at the edges, about 15 minutes, checking often during the last few minutes (no one likes an overcooked sweet roll).

Meanwhile, make the frosting: In a medium bowl, combine the cream cheese and butter and cream together using a hand mixer or fork. Add the powdered sugar and salt, mixing together until smooth. Stir in the sesame seeds and sesame oil.

Once the rolls are finished baking, remove and let cool for a few minutes. Spread the frosting over the still-warm rolls and serve immediately.

The number one breakfast request from my kids: cinnamon rolls. And the number of mornings we have enough time to make them from scratch when they ask: next to zero. Which is why Janice and I have learned to always keep a tube of premade crescent roll dough in the fridge. Not only can they be used for quick meals like pigs in a blanket, pepperoni rolls, or mini pizzas, they also make semi-homemade sweet rolls that are much better than the ready-to-go cinnamon rolls that come in a tube.

Cinnamon is classic, but I also switch the fillings on occasion, and the family's favorite is sweet rolls swirled with black sesame. They're still a breakfast that leans toward dessert, but the nutty, earthy, slightly bitter edge of the black sesame keeps them from being overly sweet. The easy recipe for homemade black sesame butter is worth your time and can be prepared well ahead of time, but if you're in a pinch, natural peanut butter makes for a great one-to-one substitute. As a finale, I like to amp up a traditional basic cream cheese frosting (the best part) with more sesame seeds and a drizzle of nutty sesame oil to match the theme and tie all the flavors together.

Bacon & Egg Sandwiches
with Maple-Braised Greens

3 tablespoons mayonnaise

1 teaspoon Tabasco, or hot sauce of choice

6 slices thick-cut bacon, cut in half

4 large eggs

Kosher salt and freshly ground black pepper

4 slices yellow American cheese

2 cups chopped kale, tough stems removed

2 tablespoons butter

2 tablespoons maple syrup

2 teaspoons apple cider vinegar

4 English muffins, split in half

MAKES 4 SANDWICHES

In a small bowl, stir together the mayo and Tabasco and set aside.

Line a plate with a paper towel and have near the stove. In a large skillet, cook the bacon slices over medium heat until crispy-chewy, flipping once, about 5 minutes on each side. Drain the bacon on the paper towel.

Use a spatula to scrape any cooked bits of bacon from the pan to one side so the eggs have a clean surface to cook. Crack the eggs into the pan and fry in the bacon fat, seasoning them with a pinch of salt and pepper. Cook until the eggs are around over-medium, with slightly runny yolks, about 2 minutes on each side. Transfer to a plate and top each egg with a slice of cheese.

Without wiping out the skillet, add the kale to the pan along with the butter. Cook the greens, stirring, until the leaves are tender, 2 to 3 minutes. Season with a pinch of salt and pepper, then add the maple syrup and vinegar. Continue cooking until almost all of the liquid has evaporated, another 1 to 2 minutes. Transfer the greens to a bowl and give the pan a quick wipe with a paper towel before returning it to the heat.

Toast the English muffins in the pan cut-side down until warmed through and lightly browned, working in batches if needed. To assemble the sandwiches, spread the mayo mixture on the bottom of each muffin, then divide the greens among the sandwiches and top with the bacon and cheesy fried egg. Serve immediately.

The inspiration for this all-in-one breakfast sandwich comes from two places: John's Roast Pork in Philly, where they put sautéed broccoli rabe on their namesake sandwich, and the famous collard green melt at Turkey and the Wolf in New Orleans. The idea is to liven up the standard breakfast muffinwich with sweet and tangy flash-sautéed greens with maple syrup and a splash of apple cider vinegar. Any leafy green will work in this recipe, though you might need to adjust the cooking time based on how hearty the green is—kale is my favorite since it softens in a hot pan in a matter of minutes, without completely losing its texture. This sandwich is also a clever way to sneak some vegetables past picky eaters. My youngest, Asher—who loves breakfast from a drive-thru as much he hates greens—gave this his seal of approval.

Eggs in Kilauea

2 tablespoons extra-virgin olive oil

2 cloves garlic, minced

2 scallions, thinly sliced, white and green parts kept separate

1 medium red bell pepper, finely diced

1 tablespoon chili garlic sauce or sambal oelek, plus more to taste

1 tablespoon tomato paste

2 teaspoons fish sauce, plus more to taste

1 teaspoon grated fresh ginger or ½ teaspoon ground ginger

1 (28-ounce) can diced tomatoes

1 teaspoon smoked paprika

½ teaspoon ground cumin

½ teaspoon freshly ground black pepper

2 tablespoons salted butter

2 tablespoons freshly grated Parmesan cheese, plus more for serving

6 large eggs

Finely chopped fresh cilantro, for garnish

Gochugaru (Korean chile flakes) or red chile flakes (optional)

Warm Hawaiian sweet rolls or sliced crusty bread, for dipping

SERVES 3 OR 4

In a large skillet with a lid, heat the oil over medium heat until shimmering. Add the garlic and scallion whites and cook, stirring often, until softened and fragrant, about 1 minute.

Stir in the bell pepper, chili garlic sauce, tomato paste, fish sauce, and ginger. Cook, stirring often, until the pepper is slightly softened, 2 to 3 minutes.

Add the canned tomatoes, smoked paprika, cumin, and black pepper. Bring the mixture to a boil, then reduce the heat to medium-low and cook, stirring occasionally and squishing the tomatoes with the back of a spoon, until the tomatoes break down and thicken into a sauce, 20 to 25 minutes.

Stir in the butter and Parmesan and season to taste with more chili garlic sauce and fish sauce if desired.

Using the back of a spoon, make 6 wells in the tomato sauce, then crack an egg into each. Cover the pan and cook until the eggs are set to taste, 2 to 3 minutes for runny yolks.

Remove the pan from the heat and sprinkle the eggs with the reserved scallion greens, chopped cilantro, more Parmesan, and gochugaru (if using) to taste. Serve with sweet rolls or crusty bread on the side for dipping.

Somewhere between shakshuka, eggs in purgatory, and sarciado, a Filipino scramble, these eggs poached in spicy, savory tomato sauce are a brunch special we serve at Tiffany's. Kilauea is an active volcano on the Big Island, so the name comes from how much the simmering sauce looks like bubbling lava. Though it's usually served for breakfast, the dish comes together so quickly it also works well for a light lunch or dinner served with warm rolls or crusty bread, which are perfect for soaking up the runny eggs and sauce. The spiciness comes from the addition of chili garlic sauce and a final sprinkle of chile flakes, both of which can be scaled up or down. Make sure to use a skillet or pan with a lid, as the eggs need to be covered to properly cook.

Pork Belly Tocino

1 cup packed light brown sugar

½ cup canned pineapple juice

¼ cup shoyu (soy sauce)

6 cloves garlic, minced

2 tablespoons distilled white vinegar

2 teaspoons freshly ground black pepper

1 teaspoon ground annatto (or ¾ teaspoon paprika + ¼ teaspoon turmeric)

3 pounds skinless pork belly, thinly sliced (about ¼ inch thick)

Neutral oil, for pan-frying

For serving

Triple-Garlic Rice (page 122)

Fried eggs

Cherry tomatoes, halved

Chile Vinegar (page 261)

SERVES 8

In a large bowl, whisk together the brown sugar, pineapple juice, shoyu, garlic, white vinegar, pepper, and annatto until the sugar is dissolved.

Place the pork belly slices in a large resealable plastic bag or shallow dish. Pour the marinade over the pork belly, making sure each slice is coated well. Seal the bag or cover the dish with plastic wrap. Marinate in the fridge for at least 24 hours, up to 3 days for the best flavor. (Marinated tocino can also be stored in the freezer for up to 3 months.)

Lightly coat the bottom of a large skillet or sauté pan with oil and heat over medium-high heat until shimmering. Add the marinated pork belly slices in a single layer without overcrowding the pan (you may need to cook in batches).

Cook the slices until the sugar in the marinade caramelizes and creates a browned crust and the slices are cooked through, 3 to 4 minutes per side.

Serve hot with garlic fried rice, fried eggs, cherry tomatoes, and chile vinegar on the side for a classic Filipino breakfast.

Tocino is sometimes referred to as Filipino bacon. But this would be like calling Prince a guy from Minnesota who plays guitar—a description that loses a lot in translation.

We had tocino on the menu at a restaurant I used to run in Wailea called Migrant. It was one of our most popular dishes by leaps and bounds, and every night for prep we would make a big batch of marinade using, among other ingredients, a certain lemon-lime soda brand that rhymes with "bright." And one day the soda salesman came to the restaurant and said, "Wow, you guys go through more [lemon-lime soda brand] than any other place I supply on Maui. How do you get people to order it?" And the answer was, well, we put it in our bacon.

This recipe contains no lemon-lime soda, however. That's because a key ingredient in tocino marinade is pineapple juice, which contains enzymes that tenderize the meat. At the restaurant we stretched our pineapple juice, which was expensive, with fizzy soda, but you don't need to do that at home (unless you really want to experience the "bright flavor"). Unlike bacon, tocino isn't cured or smoked for longevity, but marinating the pork belly in sugar, salt, and vinegar does give it that snappy bacon-like texture when it's pan-fried until browned and crispy.

Tocino can and should be enjoyed any time of day, but it's most beloved as the centerpiece of a Filipino morning staple called tosilog (tocino + garlic rice + fried egg). I like my tosilog with a few sliced cherry tomatoes for freshness and chile vinegar on the side, too, if you can swing it. Mornings don't get much better.

SALADS & VEGGIES

Sautéed Caesar
with Anchovy Croutons

For the anchovy croutons

¼ cup extra-virgin olive oil

4 slices white sandwich bread, cut in ¼-inch cubes (about 1½ cups)

6 anchovy fillets, or more to taste, roughly chopped

Kosher salt

For the stir-fry

2 medium heads romaine lettuce

1 tablespoon oyster sauce

1 teaspoon shoyu (soy sauce)

1 teaspoon sugar

1 teaspoon Worcestershire sauce

1 teaspoon toasted sesame oil

6 cloves garlic, minced

1 lemon, zested and then halved

Kosher salt and freshly ground black pepper

½ cup grated Parmesan cheese

SERVES 2 TO 4

Make the anchovy croutons: Line a plate with paper towels and have it near the stove. Place a large sauté pan or wok over medium-low heat. Add the olive oil, bread cubes, and anchovies to the skillet and stir to combine, ensuring that the bread cubes have soaked up the oil.

Cook, stirring as needed, until the croutons are golden brown and crisp on the outside, and have released their oil back into the pan, 10 to 12 minutes. Adjust the heat if the croutons are browning too fast. Transfer the fried croutons to the paper towels and sprinkle with salt. Leave any remaining oil in the pan.

Make the stir-fry: While the croutons are cooking, trim the tops and bottoms of the lettuce heads. Halve them lengthwise and then cut them crosswise into 2-inch lengths.

Return the same pan or wok (with the reserved oil) to medium-high heat. While the pan is heating, in a small bowl, whisk together the oyster sauce, shoyu, sugar, Worcestershire sauce, and sesame oil. Set the stir-fry sauce aside.

When the oil in the pan is shimmering, add the garlic and lemon zest and cook, stirring frequently, for 15 to 30 seconds, until fragrant. Add the lettuce and stir-fry for about 2 minutes, until it starts to wilt. Pour the stir-fry sauce over the lettuce and cook for another 1 to 2 minutes, until the lettuce is softened but still has some crunch. Taste and season with salt, if needed.

Transfer the lettuce (and all the pan juices) to a large plate or shallow bowl. Top with a generous amount of black pepper, the anchovy croutons, and grated Parmesan. Squeeze the lemon halves over the top just before serving.

The first place I tried stir-fried lettuce was at 8 Fat Fat 8 Bar & Grille, a dive bar in Honolulu that not-so-secretly serves some of the best Chinese food on the island. It was at the end of a long, drink-filled night, and while questionable decisions were made (see: tequila shots), ordering the garlicky, tender-crisp, wok-kissed lettuce was not one of them.

The traditional Chinese version of this dish is made with iceberg lettuce, but 8 Fat Fat 8's chef used romaine instead, cut into short spears and cooked with shoyu, plus an aggressive amount of minced garlic and chiles. That combination made me think of Caesar salad, and this lightning strike was the result: a savory romaine stir-fry with bold flavors and a snappy crunch, set off with fragrant anchovy croutons, grated Parmesan, and a brightening squeeze of lemon. Much like you'd present a salad alongside an entrée, enjoy this as a side with rice and meat dishes.

Foolproof Pineapple Slaw

3 cups thinly sliced green cabbage (9 ounces; see Note)

1 cup thinly sliced red cabbage (3 ounces)

½ cup grated carrot (2 ounces)

Kosher salt

1 heaping teaspoon plus 1 tablespoon sugar

½ (20-ounce) can crushed pineapple with juice

½ cup mayonnaise

Grated zest of ½ lime

2 teaspoons fresh lime juice

¼ teaspoon ground white or freshly ground black pepper

MAKES ABOUT 4 CUPS

In a large bowl, combine both cabbages and the carrot. Sprinkle with 1 heaping teaspoon of salt and the 1 heaping teaspoon of sugar and toss to combine. Let sit for 15 to 20 minutes.

Gently press down on the mixture and pour off any liquid from the bottom of the bowl. Add the pineapple, mayo, the remaining 1 tablespoon sugar, lime zest, lime juice, and pepper. Stir well to combine, then taste and season with more salt as needed (keep in mind the slaw will taste less salty once it's chilled).

Cover the bowl and refrigerate for at least 1 hour (up to overnight) before serving.

This recipe is as battle-tested as it gets. When I worked at the now-closed Aloha Mixed Plate in Lahaina, one of my tasks would be to whip up fifty-pound batches of this very slaw to be served with the kālua pig we made for the nightly luau barbecue. Rare was the night in which we didn't go through most, if not all, of that fifty pounds.

The reason pineapple, specifically canned pineapple, is a great addition to coleslaw is that it delivers several of the flavors you need at once: It's sweet, slightly tart, and refreshing. You really don't need much else besides mayo and pepper. My lone addition here is some lime juice and zest for added freshness. Whatever you do, never, never skip the cardinal rule for all coleslaw-making: a quick salt-and-sugar cure to draw out excess moisture from the cabbage, which ensures your slaw stays crunchy-crisp, even through several fire dancer performances.

Note: You can substitute one 14-ounce bag coleslaw mix for the cabbages and carrot.

Coriander Carrot Salad

2 pounds carrots (about 6 large carrots), peeled and coarsely grated (or julienned)

½ cup finely chopped fresh cilantro leaves plus 1 tablespoon finely chopped cilantro stems

3 tablespoons distilled white vinegar, plus more to taste

4 teaspoons sugar, plus more to taste

2 teaspoons kosher salt, plus more to taste

6 cloves garlic, minced or grated

1½ teaspoons ground coriander

1½ teaspoons smoked paprika

¾ teaspoon freshly ground black pepper

½ teaspoon gochugaru (Korean chile flakes) or red chile flakes to taste

¼ cup avocado oil

SERVES 6 TO 8

In a large bowl, toss together the carrots, cilantro leaves, vinegar, sugar, and salt until combined. Set aside.

In a small heatproof bowl, combine the garlic, cilantro stems, ground coriander, smoked paprika, black pepper, and gochugaru.

In a small saucepan, heat the oil over medium-high heat until it just begins to smoke. Remove the pan from the heat, then stir the oil into the bowl of spices and herbs (careful, it will sizzle). Immediately pour the hot seasoned oil over the carrot mixture, tossing to mix.

Cover and refrigerate until ready to serve. While the salad is ready to eat immediately, it does taste better chilled overnight.

Morkovcha is a tangy and slightly sweet coriander-carrot kimchi that originated from ethnic Koreans living in the former Soviet Union. The reason I've become obsessed with this dish, cultural geography aside, is that it's a super-easy and flavorful vegetable side that shows off a cool cooking technique: infusing sizzling oil with spices and aromatics and then pouring them over raw shredded carrots to soften and flash-cook them. Though there's no fermentation involved, adding vinegar does help keep the salad for several days in the fridge. Use it like you would another pickley, side-salady dish, either as a garnish or condiment or just enjoyed on its own.

Avocado-Papaya Salad
with Papaya Seed Vinaigrette

2 ripe medium papayas

For the dressing

2 tablespoons Dijon mustard

1 tablespoon apple cider vinegar

1 tablespoon fresh lime juice

2 teaspoons honey

1 large shallot, finely chopped

1 cup avocado oil

Kosher salt and freshly ground black pepper

For the salad

2 large Hass avocados, cut into ½-inch cubes

1 cup halved cherry tomatoes

1 large seedless cucumber, cut into ½-inch chunks

Handful of mint leaves, roughly chopped

SERVES 4

Peel and seed the papayas and reserve about 2 tablespoons of the seeds for the dressing. Cut the papaya into ½-inch cubes. Measure out ¼ cup for the dressing and set the rest aside for the salad.

Make the dressing: Rinse the reserved papaya seeds under cold water to remove any excess pulp attached to them.

In a blender or food processor, combine the rinsed seeds, the ¼ cup papaya cubes, the mustard, vinegar, lime juice, honey, and shallot. Blend until smooth and creamy.

With the machine running on low speed, gradually drizzle in the avocado oil until the dressing emulsifies and thickens. Season with salt and pepper to taste. Transfer the dressing to a container and refrigerate until ready to use (it will keep for 2 to 3 days).

Assemble the salad: In a large salad bowl, combine the remaining papaya cubes, the avocados, tomatoes, cucumber, and mint. Gently toss to mix.

To serve, divide the salad onto individual plates or a large serving platter. Drizzle the papaya seed dressing over the salad just before serving.

As the saying goes, what grows together goes together, and in this case, that wisdom is applied to two of Hawai'i's year-round tropical fruits: avocado and papaya. This simple buttery and sweet salad is common in the Caribbean, but given the amount of papaya and avocado trees growing in yards here, it makes sense from a Hawaiian perspective, too. The papayas in Hawai'i tend to be larger than the ones on the mainland, so if you're using a Hawaiian-grown papaya, you might only need one. And don't throw away the seeds. They add a mild peppery flavor and act as emulsifier when blended into the dressing, a simple mustard vinaigrette that you'll see on the menu at many resorts. When it comes to avocados, certain varieties of Hawai'i-grown ones are special: ultrabuttery, never bland, and always full of flavor. If you're on the mainland, use the largest Hass avocados you can find and make sure they are properly ripe (ripe avocados give slightly to firm, gentle pressure but don't feel mushy).

Avocado "Tataki"
with Finadene

½ small sweet onion, finely diced

¼ cup calamansi juice (see Note), fresh or frozen

3 tablespoons shoyu (soy sauce)

2 tablespoons bonito flakes or ½ teaspoon mushroom bouillon powder (optional)

1 large tomato, halved

1 tablespoon minced fresh ginger

1 tablespoon extra-virgin olive oil, plus more for drizzling

2 avocados, halved and pitted, skin on

Kosher salt

1 tablespoon finely minced fresh basil, mint, or shiso

Freshly ground black pepper

SERVES 4

Put the onion in a sieve and rinse under cold water to mellow its sharpness slightly. Set aside to drain.

In a small blender or food processor, combine the calamansi juice, shoyu, and bonito flakes (if using). Squeeze the juice and pulp of the tomato halves into the blender, discarding the skin. Blend until smooth. In a small bowl, stir together the onion and ginger and set aside.

In a large skillet, heat the olive oil over medium-high heat. Sprinkle each cut avocado half with a big pinch of salt. Once the oil starts to smoke, add the avocados, cut-side down. Cook, undisturbed, until nicely browned, 2 to 3 minutes. Transfer to a plate and let cool.

Use a paring knife to thinly slice the avocado lengthwise while they're still in their skin. Then use a spoon to carefully scoop out each avocado half, trying to keep the avocado as intact as possible. Place each half seared-side up in a wide bowl or rimmed plate, then use the spoon to gently flatten and fan out the sliced avocado on the plate. Divide the onion-ginger mixture among the avocado halves, then spoon on equal amounts of the shoyu-citrus dressing. Top with the minced herbs, a drizzle of olive oil, and a pinch of black pepper. Serve immediately.

At Tiffany's, one of our most popular dishes is freshly caught hamachi sashimi served over our take on finadene, a fragrant, doctored-up shoyu mixture that originates from Guam. The dressing is so good, you could pour it over an old shoe and be happy. So even if someone doesn't eat raw fish, I don't want them to miss out on the experience. The best vegetable alternative I've found is to take a ripe avocado and pan-sear it "tataki-style" (cooked quickly over very high heat) on one side. The searing has a few benefits: It warms the fat in the avocado and makes it taste even creamier, and it adds a delicious slightly charred aroma. The dried bonito flakes (found at Japanese or Asian markets, or online) blended into the sauce add a wonderful umami bass note to the dressing, but they're not strictly required. If you'd like to make this dish vegan, simply omit them or substitute with a pinch of umami-rich mushroom bouillon powder.

Note: If you're unable to find calamansi juice, use equal parts lemon and lime juice with some orange zest (see the Toyomansi recipe, page 256, for specifics).

Okoy Fritters

1¼ cups potato starch

½ cup plus 2 tablespoons all-purpose flour

1 tablespoon ground annatto (or 2¼ teaspoons paprika + ¾ teaspoon turmeric)

1 teaspoon kosher salt, plus more as needed

½ teaspoon freshly ground black pepper

6 ounces julienned peeled green papaya (about ½ green papaya) or green beans cut into 1½-inch-long matchsticks

6 ounces julienned peeled sweet potato (about ½ medium-large sweet potato)

2 medium carrots, julienned

1 small red onion, thinly sliced

Neutral oil, for frying

Okoy Dipping Sauce (recipe follows), for serving

SERVES 8

In a large bowl, whisk together the potato starch, flour, annatto, salt, and pepper with 1½ cups cold water until a smooth batter forms.

In another large bowl, toss together the green papaya, sweet potato, carrots, and red onion until evenly mixed. Set aside.

Line a baking sheet with paper towels and have it near the stove. Pour 1 inch of oil into a wok or large Dutch oven and heat over medium-high heat to 350°F on a deep-fry thermometer.

Add about ½ cup of the vegetable mixture to a large metal ladle, then using a measuring cup, spoon ¼ cup of the batter mixture directly on top of the vegetables. Gently slide this mixture off the ladle into the oil and fry, flipping once, until golden brown and crispy on both sides, 3 to 4 minutes total. Working in batches so as not to crowd the pan, fry the rest of the fritters, adjusting the heat as needed. Drain the finished fritters on the paper towels and season with a pinch of salt. Serve immediately with the dipping sauce.

recipe continues →

Okoy (or ukoy) are crispy Filipino fritters made from julienned vegetables, shrimp, and a thin starchy batter that binds everything together and turns ferociously crunchy when baptized in hot oil. As with any fried food, they're a big hit at parties. Most days, however, I end up getting them at the Filipino grocery stores near Wailuku when I'm shopping for produce—the aunties usually have a heat lamp near the register where you'll find these golden beauties sunbathing.

Growing up in Hilo, I don't remember frying okoy at family parties, but we did fry a lot of tempura, which is probably why the vegetable okoy our ohana makes now falls somewhere between traditional okoy and Japanese kakiage. Here, I use potato starch in the batter, which produces a stretchy, slightly chewy fritter that's light and delicate with a superior crispiness. I also prefer to shallow-fry these like latkes, which requires less oil than a full deep-fry. The easiest way to do this is to use a metal ladle as a building station: Add a handful of shredded veggies to the bowl of the ladle, spoon batter on top, then carefully slide the mixture from the ladle directly into the hot oil.

Consider the vegetables included here suggestions, as you can substitute any firm vegetable as long as it doesn't contain too much moisture and can be julienned into thin strips using a vegetable peeler or knife: parsnips, bell peppers, bean sprouts, or cabbage are all good options. Whatever you do, don't skip the vinegar dipping sauce. A freshly fried okoy without a splash of vinegar is like a sundae without hot fudge.

Okoy Dipping Sauce MAKES ABOUT 1 CUP

¾ cup cane vinegar or distilled white vinegar

1 tablespoon fish sauce

3 cloves garlic, minced

1 teaspoon chili garlic sauce or sambal oelek, plus more to taste

½ teaspoon freshly ground black pepper

In a small bowl, stir together vinegar, fish sauce, garlic, chili garlic sauce, and pepper with 3 tablespoons water.

The Komine ohana—our ride-or-die family. From raising kids and sharing meals to laughs, bottles, and workouts, together we've grown closer and stronger every rep of the way.

Roasted Mushrooms "Escargot"

1 pound cremini or white mushrooms, halved lengthwise if large

2 tablespoons minced anchovies

2 tablespoons extra-virgin olive oil

3 cloves garlic, minced

2 tablespoons minced shallot or sweet onion

1 teaspoon grated lemon zest

Kosher salt and freshly ground pepper

4 tablespoons (½ stick) cold butter, sliced

1 tablespoon finely chopped fresh flat-leaf parsley

2 teaspoons fresh lemon juice

Freshly grated Parmesan cheese (optional)

Toasted French bread slices, for serving

SERVES 2 TO 4

Preheat the oven to 425°F.

In a large ovenproof skillet or roasting pan, toss the mushrooms with the anchovies, olive oil, garlic, shallot, lemon zest, and a big pinch of salt and pepper. Top with the butter slices and transfer to the oven.

Roast, undisturbed, until the mushrooms are tender and lightly browned, 15 to 20 minutes.

Stir in the parsley and lemon juice. Sprinkle with Parmesan (if using) and serve warm with toast.

This is loosely based on a dish you'll find at Side Street Inn in Honolulu. Depending on who you ask, Side Street Inn is either a local bar with an amazing food menu or a great restaurant where you can have bargain whiskey-gingers after work. Either way, they know a thing or two about the best drinking foods, and their garlic butter mushrooms are among their best offerings. I prefer roasting mushrooms in the oven to sautéing for convenience, but if you don't want to turn on the oven, you can simply cook mushrooms in a dry pan over medium heat until they've released all their water and the pan turns dry again, then add the rest of the ingredients.

I call these "escargot" mushrooms because they're seasoned similarly to the French snail dish, with chopped anchovies adding a touch of brininess to the traditional garlic herb butter. If you'd like to make this dish vegan, just omit the anchovies and replace the butter with margarine or vegan butter.

Zucchini Jun

1 large zucchini, sliced into ¼-inch-thick rounds

2 tablespoons shoyu (soy sauce)

1 tablespoon sugar

2 teaspoons toasted sesame oil

Kosher salt

2 large eggs, lightly beaten

All-purpose flour, for dredging

Neutral oil, for pan-frying

Jun Sauce (recipe follows), for serving

SERVES 2

On a large plate or small rimmed tray, arrange the zucchini slices in a single layer. Use a fork to puka (poke) small holes all over the zucchini slices, which will help them soak up the marinade.

In a small bowl, whisk together the shoyu, sugar, sesame oil, and a pinch of salt until the sugar is dissolved. Pour the marinade evenly over the zucchini and let sit for 10 minutes, turning the slices halfway through.

Meanwhile, add a few handfuls of flour to a plate for dredging.

Line a baking sheet with paper towels and have it near the stove. In a large skillet, add just enough neutral oil to coat the bottom of the pan and heat over medium-high heat. Once the oil is shimmering, start the dredging process: One by one, coat the marinated zucchini slices in the flour, shaking off any excess, dip them into the beaten eggs, and add them to the skillet, working in batches so you don't overcrowd the pan.

Cook the zucchini until the bottom edges turn lightly golden brown, about 1 minute. Flip and cook for another minute until golden brown on the other side. Add more oil between batches if necessary. Place the fried zucchini on the paper towels to drain. Serve immediately with the dipping sauce.

recipe continues →

In my first book, *Cook Real Hawai'i,* I have an eggplant recipe that riffs on local-style meat jun, a homestyle dish that could best be described as country-fried bulgogi. Originally Korean, jun is more of a technique than a dish, which is why it's helpful to think of it as a verb rather than a noun—as in, you can *jun* pretty much anything.

Here it's slices of zucchini that are getting the jun treatment: a quick dip in a basic bulgogi-esque marinade, then a coat of egg and flour that will turn browned and crispy when fried in a thin layer of oil. Make sure to take the time to *puka* (Hawaiian for "poke holes in") the zucchini first so that it soaks up the seasoning and turns custardy during its short fry.

With the savory-sweet, slightly creamy gochujang dipping sauce, this jun is a perfect appetizer, or you can turn it into a one-bowl meal by stacking the zucchini over rice, drizzling with sauce, and garnishing with scallions or whatever pickles or condiments are on hand.

Jun Sauce MAKES ABOUT ½ CUP

- 2 tablespoons shoyu (soy sauce)
- 2 tablespoons distilled white vinegar
- 1 tablespoon mayonnaise
- 1 tablespoon sugar
- 1 tablespoon gochujang (Korean chile paste)
- 1 tablespoon toasted sesame seeds

In a small bowl, whisk together the shoyu, vinegar, mayo, sugar, gochujang, and sesame seeds until combined.

Maui born and raised chef Kyle Kawakami with his son, Tai

Crispy Chili-Garlic Cauliflower

For the cauliflower

3 tablespoons extra-virgin olive oil, plus more for the baking sheet

2 large eggs, lightly beaten

2 teaspoons gochugaru (Korean chile flakes) or red chile flakes

½ teaspoon kosher salt, plus more as needed

½ teaspoon freshly ground black pepper

½ teaspoon ground cinnamon

½ teaspoon ground turmeric

1 head cauliflower, cut into florets about the size of a Ping-Pong ball

¾ cup panko bread crumbs

2 teaspoons toasted sesame seeds

4 cloves garlic, minced

1 jalapeño, seeded and finely chopped

1 tablespoon minced fresh ginger

3 scallions, chopped, white and green parts kept separate

For the chili garlic glaze

¼ cup honey

3 tablespoons chili garlic sauce

2 tablespoons extra-virgin olive oil

SERVES 4

Cook the cauliflower: Preheat the oven to 425°F. Place a full-sized baking sheet in the oven to preheat while the oven comes to temp.

In a large bowl, whisk together the olive oil, eggs, gochugaru, salt, pepper, cinnamon, and turmeric. Add the cauliflower florets and toss to coat in the egg mixture. Add the panko and toss to coat once more. Add the sesame seeds, garlic, jalapeño, fresh ginger, and the scallion whites. Gently toss to combine.

Carefully remove the preheated baking sheet from the oven (you can also line the sheet pan with parchment paper first for easier cleanup). Drizzle with olive oil. Spread the florets onto it so they're in a single, evenly spaced layer, then sprinkle them with a few pinches of salt.

Bake until the florets are golden-brown and crispy, 30 to 40 minutes, stirring every 10 minutes or so.

Meanwhile, make the chili garlic glaze: In a small saucepan, stir together the honey, chili garlic sauce, and olive oil and cook over medium-low heat until heated through and fragrant, 2 to 3 minutes. Remove from the heat.

Drizzle the crispy cauliflower with the glaze and garnish with the reserved scallion greens. Serve immediately.

Here's a secret to eating more vegetables: They taste better when they're seasoned. I've never known anyone who got excited over a plain head of cauliflower, but there is a reason so many restaurants (mine included) sell a lot of roasted cauliflower, and that's because it takes to attention-grabbing seasonings better than most anything else from the produce aisle.

This loosely Chinese-Indian recipe involves a two-step process that yields a dish with impressive depth of flavor. I'm making the maximalist version here, but the spice and aromatics are flexible based on what you have. First, toss the florets with oil, eggs, bread crumbs, and spices to form a thin dredge that turns crunchy and fragrant in the oven. For truly crispy cauliflower, make sure your florets are trimmed into a roughly uniform size, and preheat the baking sheet in the oven so the cauliflower starts browning on contact. While the vegetables are roasting, use that time to make a quick hot honey glaze to drizzle over the cauliflower before serving.

Asparagus Rumaki

1 pound thin asparagus spears

2 tablespoons oyster sauce

1 teaspoon cornstarch

1 teaspoon sugar

½ teaspoon chicken bouillon powder

1 tablespoon neutral oil

¼ pound thick-cut bacon, cut into 2-inch pieces

1 (8-ounce) can sliced water chestnuts, drained

4 cloves garlic, minced

Freshly ground black pepper

SERVES 2 TO 4

Trim the asparagus by bending each spear and finding the place where it snaps (usually the bottom third), which will keep only the tender sections for the stir-fry. Slice the asparagus spears into 2-inch lengths on a diagonal and set aside.

In a small bowl, whisk together the oyster sauce, cornstarch, sugar, and bouillon powder with 1 tablespoon water until smooth. Set aside.

In a large skillet or wok, heat the oil over medium heat until shimmering. Add the sliced bacon and stir-fry until browned and crispy around the edges, 5 to 6 minutes.

Increase the heat to medium-high. Add the asparagus, water chestnuts, and garlic and stir-fry until the asparagus are tender but still a little crisp, 4 to 5 minutes. Give the reserved sauce one more stir to mix, then add to the skillet, tossing to combine. Stir-fry for another minute until the sauce has thickened and clings to the ingredients. Season with a big pinch of black pepper, then remove the pan from the heat. Serve immediately.

Rumaki is an old-school appetizer whose popularity can be traced back to the tiki craze that swept through Hawaiʻi (and everywhere else in the United States) during the 1960s. Originally made with chicken livers, these days you'll often find it with water chestnuts wrapped in bacon. I love the combination of the two—salty bacon and crisp water chestnuts—but I'm not a fan of the meticulous task of wrapping, whether that's rumaki, lumpia, presents at Christmas, etc. Here I'm sidestepping the work but not the flavor, by turning a great party appetizer into a great stir-fry. If you can't find asparagus in season, fresh green beans or sliced half-moons of zucchini are nice substitutes as well.

Teriyaki Potatoes

1 pound Yukon Gold potatoes (4 or 5 medium potatoes), peeled and cut into 1½-inch pieces

Kosher salt

2 tablespoons neutral oil

3 tablespoons shoyu (soy sauce)

3 tablespoons agave syrup or maple syrup

1 clove garlic, minced or grated

1 teaspoon toasted sesame oil

1 tablespoon toasted sesame seeds

½ teaspoon gochugaru (Korean chile flakes) or red chile flakes

SERVES 4

In a large microwave-safe bowl, toss the potatoes with a big pinch of salt. Microwave for 3 minutes, stir, then microwave for another 3 minutes (the potatoes don't need to be fully tender, just cooked enough that you can just pierce them with a fork).

In a large skillet, heat the oil over medium-high heat until shimmering. While the oil is heating, in a small bowl, whisk together the shoyu, syrup, and garlic. Add the potatoes to the pan and cook, stirring, until golden and crispy, 5 to 7 minutes.

Pour the sauce over the potatoes and stir to coat. Continue to cook, stirring often, until the sauce is reduced and clings to the potatoes, another 2 to 3 minutes. Remove from the heat and stir in the sesame oil, then sprinkle with the sesame seeds and gochugaru. Serve hot.

There is a lot of crossover between Japanese and Korean cuisine in Hawai'i and the reason has to do with immigration patterns. By the time Korean immigrants started to arrive to work at the sugar plantations in the 1900s, much larger groups of Japanese immigrants had already dominated the plantation workforce for decades. That meant that newly arrived Koreans in Hawai'i often found themselves cooking with Japanese ingredients from Japanese-owned stores, which was by far the closest approximation they could get to what they would find at home. So even though these sweet soy-glazed potatoes eaten in Hawai'i have a familiar Japanese name, they share a lot of culinary DNA with the Korean dish gamja jorim (namely: the foundational local combo of shoyu and sugar).

Whatever this dish is called, I also call it fantastic, and it might be my favorite banchan (side dish) ever. Cutting the potatoes into small chunks and steaming them in the microwave saves on cooking time. Alternatively, you can use leftover boiled potatoes and skip straight to the pan-frying and glazing step. Using sweet potatoes is a nice variation as well. Enjoy these as a side or just something to nibble on with beer.

Boursin Mashed Potatoes

2 pounds russet potatoes (3 to 4 potatoes), peeled and quartered

Kosher salt

½ cup half-and-half

4 tablespoons (½ stick) butter, cubed

2 cloves garlic, grated

1 (5.3-ounce) package Garlic & Fine Herbs Boursin cheese (or any flavor Boursin)

Ground white pepper or freshly ground black pepper

2 tablespoons minced fresh chives or parsley (optional)

SERVES 6

Place the peeled and quartered potatoes in a large pot, cover with cold water, and add a big pinch of salt. Bring to a boil over medium-high heat. Reduce the heat to a simmer and cook until the potatoes are fork-tender, 15 to 20 minutes.

While the potatoes are cooking, in a small saucepan, stir together the half-and-half, butter, and garlic and warm over low heat until the butter is melted. Keep warm until ready to use.

Once the potatoes are cooked, drain well and return them to the pot. Mash them using a potato masher or fork until they're broken down into marble-size chunks. Add the Boursin cheese to the mashed potatoes while they're still warm. Mix until the cheese is fully incorporated and melted. Gradually pour in the warm butter mixture while continuing to mix the potatoes until they're creamy and smooth. Taste and season with salt and white pepper as needed.

Transfer to a serving bowl or dish, sprinkle on the chives (if using), and serve warm.

We always run prime rib specials on weekends at Tiffany's and part of the fun for the kitchen is rotating through different potato dishes we've come up with over the years. These cheese-enriched potatoes are easily the winner of the bunch. I'm not sure how the French do it, but there's something about the texture of Boursin cheese that when mixed in with warm mashed potatoes makes them silky, creamy, and stretchy all at once while adding a delicious herb-garlic flavor, too. It's a no-brainer served with the Prime Rib Roast with Shoyu Jus (page 223), but it's also become my go-to mashed potato recipe whenever some smushed spuds are required.

Pocho Bean Salad

1 shallot or ½ small red onion, finely chopped

3 cloves garlic, grated

3 bay leaves, broken in half

2 tablespoons red wine vinegar

Grated zest and juice of ½ lemon

2 (15-ounce) cans beans, such as kidney, cannellini, navy, and/or chickpeas, rinsed and well drained

½ cup finely chopped soft herbs, such as flat-leaf parsley, basil, mint, cilantro, and/or dill

¼ cup extra-virgin olive oil

1 teaspoon smoked paprika

1 teaspoon gochugaru (Korean chile flakes) or red chile flakes

Kosher salt and freshly ground black pepper

SERVES 4 TO 6

In a small bowl, combine the shallot, garlic, bay leaves, vinegar, lemon zest, and lemon juice and let sit for 5 minutes.

Meanwhile, in a large bowl, toss together the beans, herbs, olive oil, smoked paprika, and gochugaru. Season generously with salt and black pepper.

Add the shallot-vinegar mixture to the bean mixture and gently stir to combine. Taste and season with more salt and pepper as needed. Cover and refrigerate for at least 2 hours before serving.

Portuguese cuisine—what you might hear called "pocho" food locally—has a strong influence in Hawai'i. The most iconic Portuguese recipes for me are pickled onions, which is a mainstay in local fridges and restaurants, and vinha d'alhos, a tangy braised pork dish. The common thread in both is a healthy glug of vinegar and loads of fresh garlic. This recipe takes the seasoning blueprint and applies it to a punchy bean salad that I love on hot days, or those days when you just don't want to turn on any appliance in the kitchen.

If you're worried about ending up with one of those mushy, bland bean salads you sometimes find at potlucks, this is far from it. Start with room-temperature canned beans and rinse and drain them in a colander, as the starchy liquid can make the salad soggy. And while it's perfectly fine to chill the prepared salad overnight, a few hours in the fridge is plenty to let the ingredients meld. Just be sure to let the salad sit out at room temperature for a bit before serving—a too-cold bean salad means muted flavors. Also keep in mind that since beans absorb salt as they sit, it's best to taste and season a second time right before serving.

Note: Bulk this salad up by mixing in a drained can of tuna or some firm, crumbly cheese like feta.

Sesame-Tofu Green Beans

1 pound green beans, trimmed and cut into 1-inch pieces

Kosher salt

¼ cup toasted sesame seeds

8 ounces (½ block) medium-firm tofu, firmly pressed and patted dry

2 tablespoons mayonnaise

1 tablespoon shiro (white) miso

2 teaspoons fresh lemon juice

2 teaspoons maple syrup

1 teaspoon shoyu (soy sauce)

SERVES 4

In a medium saucepan, combine the green beans, ½ cup water, and several big pinches of salt. Cover and cook over medium-high heat, stirring occasionally, until the green beans are tender but still have a slight snap to them, 15 to 18 minutes. Drain well.

Using a mortar and pestle, a spice grinder, or a plastic bag and a rolling pin on a flat surface, crush the sesame seeds until roughly ground.

Add the sesame seeds to a medium bowl. Crumble the tofu into small pieces with your hands and add to the bowl along with the green beans, mayo, miso, lemon juice, maple syrup, and shoyu. Mix thoroughly. Taste and season with salt as needed.

The salad can be served warm or cold, but during warm weather it's best chilled in the fridge for at least 1 hour.

This is a riff on the Japanese side dish shira-ae, a vegan-friendly salad made with fresh green beans, creamy tofu, nutty toasted sesame seeds, and savory miso paste. It can also be made with other blanched green vegetables, such as snap peas, baby broccolini, thin asparagus, or fresh spinach—or whatever else is currently wasting away in your vegetable crisper.

Broccoli Banchan

- Kosher salt
- 1 pound broccoli, cut into florets
- 4 teaspoons toasted sesame oil
- 3 cloves garlic, grated, or 1 teaspoon garlic powder
- Freshly ground black pepper
- 4 teaspoons toasted sesame seeds

SERVES 4

Add a few big pinches of salt to a large pot of water and bring to a boil. Add the broccoli and cook until the florets are bright green, 2 to 3 minutes. Drain in a colander and rinse under cold water until cool. Pat dry and transfer to a large bowl.

In a small bowl, whisk together 1 teaspoon salt, the sesame oil, garlic, and a few pinches of black pepper. Pour the mixture over the broccoli and toss to coat. Add the sesame seeds and toss once more. Taste and adjust with more salt and pepper if needed. Serve immediately.

Tin Roof line cook and avid hunter and fisherman Anthony Aboy with his wife, Princess, and their kids

You'll often find this blanched broccoli side dish at Korean BBQ restaurants, and I'm always blown away by how delicious it is for such an elemental recipe. Properly salting this dish is crucial for bringing out the flavors of garlic and sesame seeds, so don't be afraid to taste and season a few times as you toss the broccoli with sesame oil and garlic.

Spicy Garlic Cucumbers

- 1 pound seedless cucumbers, sliced into ½-inch-thick rounds
- 1 teaspoon kosher salt
- 1 tablespoon gochujang (Korean chile paste)
- 1 tablespoon distilled white vinegar
- 1 tablespoon toasted sesame oil
- 2 teaspoons gochugaru (Korean chile flakes) or red chile flakes
- 2 teaspoons shoyu (soy sauce)
- 2 teaspoons sugar
- 2 cloves garlic, minced or grated

SERVES 4

In a medium bowl, toss the cucumbers with the salt, then transfer to a colander and set a timer for 20 minutes. Set the colander in the sink to drain while you make the dressing.

While the cucumbers are curing, in a medium bowl, whisk together the gochujang, vinegar, sesame oil, gochugaru, shoyu, sugar, and garlic.

After 20 minutes, add the cucumbers to the dressing and toss to coat. Serve immediately.

Melissa Padilla (center), food stylist and creative, with her husband, Kaleo, and their family

Known as *oi muchim* in Korean, this quick-pickled cucumber side dish is crunchy, spicy, and refreshing. It's great as a snack on its own, but it also works as a tangy and snappy contrast to any kind of grilled or stir-fried meat.

NOODLES & RICE

Deluxe Cheeseburger Mac

1 pound lean ground beef (90/10)
½ large yellow onion, chopped
6 cloves garlic, minced
3 tablespoons butter
3 tablespoons all-purpose flour
1 tablespoon Worcestershire sauce
½ teaspoon freshly ground black pepper
1 cup half-and-half or whole milk
3 cups (12 ounces) macaroni
2 cups low-sodium beef broth
1 (14.5-ounce) can diced tomatoes
1 tablespoon yellow mustard
1 tablespoon ketchup
6 slices yellow American cheese, torn into small pieces, or 4 ounces Velveeta cheese, cut into cubes
1 cup freshly grated Cheddar cheese
Dill pickle chips, for serving

SERVES 6

Heat a large skillet over medium-high heat. Add the ground beef and brown, stirring often to break up the meat, until no pink remains, 6 to 8 minutes.

Add the onion and garlic and cook, stirring often, until softened, 3 to 4 minutes.

Stir in the butter, flour, Worcestershire sauce, and pepper until combined. After the flour has absorbed some of the liquid, add the half-and-half and stir to combine, making sure there are no lumps in the sauce. Stir in the macaroni, beef broth, diced tomatoes, mustard, and ketchup. Bring to a boil. Reduce the heat to medium-low, cover, and simmer until the pasta is tender, or slightly less if you prefer it al dente, 10 to 12 minutes.

Stir in the American and Cheddar cheeses until melted and a thick sauce forms. Serve warm with a side of pickles.

My older brother and I cooked a lot of Filipino food growing up, but on days between sinigang and adobo, our favorite thing to make for dinner was a haole-born treat: Hamburger Helper. If you ranked all the dishes I've ever cooked by how often I made them, HH's red box would crack the top five. Cheeseburger macaroni is still a fixture in the Simeon house, for the same reason now as back when I was little: because there's always a block of ground beef in the freezer.

My lone beef (ha) with cheeseburger mac from the box is that it never tastes "cheeseburgery" enough, which can be fixed by a few "doctor-ups," like adding diced tomatoes, a mix of quality American cheese and Cheddar, and a squirt of yellow mustard and ketchup. If you're going through that effort, you might as well make a basic roux, too, which produces a creamier and richer mac without difficulty. I've heard of some people chopping up pickles and mixing it into the pot, but I'm an advocate of alternating bites of cheeseburger mac with dill pickle chips on the side, like banchan.

Palabucatini

Kosher salt

1 pound bucatini

1 pound heads-on jumbo shrimp

1 tablespoon neutral oil

1 teaspoon ground annatto (or ¾ teaspoon paprika + ¼ teaspoon turmeric)

1 pound ground pork

½ medium yellow onion, chopped

6 cloves garlic, minced

4 teaspoons fish sauce

1 tablespoon oyster sauce

2 teaspoons chicken bouillon powder

1 teaspoon sugar

2 tablespoons cornstarch

1 large egg, lightly beaten

Bring a large pot of salted water to a boil. Add the bucatini and cook according to the package directions for al dente. Drain and set aside.

Meanwhile, remove the heads and peel the shells from the shrimp and set aside. Finely chop the peeled raw shrimp so it's roughly the same texture as ground pork and place in the fridge for later.

In a large saucepan, heat the oil over medium-high heat until shimmering. Add the shrimp heads and shells and stir-fry for 2 to 3 minutes, until they turn from gray to pink-red in color. Remove the pan from the heat.

In a blender or food processor, combine the cooked shells, annatto, and 4 cups water. Blend until smooth, then return the liquid to the saucepan.

Bring to a boil, then remove from the heat. Once the stock has cooled slightly, pour it through a fine-mesh sieve to remove the shrimp shells. Transfer the stock to another container and wipe out the saucepan.

recipe and ingredients continue →

Sometimes greatness happens by accident. This dish came about years ago during a cooking event I did at the Grand Wailea with other local chefs. We were looking to do a version of a Filipino dish called pancit palabok, a saucy carbonara-like noodle dish made with garlic, pork, shrimp, and eggs. We couldn't get ahold of the traditional rice noodles in time, so we substituted bucatini, long strands of dried pasta with a tiny hole (puka, in Hawaiian) running down the middle. Thus: palabucatini was born.

As it turned out, bucatini was ideal for soaking up the flavorful gravy, which we made from egg-thickened shrimp stock. It was the most delicious palabok I've tasted—rich with pork and shrimp, a little funky from fish and oyster sauce, and deeply savory from the hearty, garlicky annatto-tinged sauce the noodles are tossed in—and has since become my favorite way to make the dish. Even counting the time it takes to make shrimp stock, this showstopper comes together in less than an hour, or you can prepare the sauce in advance and freeze it for faster assembly.

At its most maximalist, traditional pancit palabok is decorated with a medley of toppings like hard-boiled eggs, crushed pork rinds, sliced scallions, fried garlic, and Parmesan, plus lemon wedges to squeeze over the top. Feel free to dress these noodles up with as many or as few of them as you like.

For serving (optional but encouraged)

2 hard-boiled eggs, finely chopped

½ cup finely crushed pork rinds and/or shrimp chips

¼ cup freshly grated Parmesan cheese

¼ cup thinly sliced scallions

2 tablespoons Fried Garlic (page 30)

Freshly ground black pepper

Lemon wedges, for squeezing

SERVES 4

In the same saucepan over medium-high heat, add the ground pork and stir-fry until browned and cooked through, 4 to 5 minutes. Transfer the pork from the pan to a small bowl using a slotted spoon, leaving the fat in the pan, or draining off all but 1 tablespoon of the fat, if desired.

Return the pan to medium-high heat and add the onion, garlic, and chopped shrimp. Cook, stirring frequently, until the shrimp turn pink, about 1 minute, then return the cooked pork. Stir in the fish sauce, oyster sauce, bouillon powder, and sugar. Once everything is combined, add the reserved shrimp stock and bring to a boil. Reduce the heat to a simmer and continue cooking, skimming off any foam that forms on the surface, until the sauce has reduced by about one-third, 10 to 15 minutes. (At this point, the sauce can be cooled, transferred to an airtight container, and stored in the freezer for up to 2 months.)

In a small bowl, whisk together the cornstarch, egg, and 3 tablespoons cold water until smooth. Drizzle into the simmering broth while stirring and continue cooking until the sauce is thickened, 1 to 2 minutes.

Finally, add the cooked bucatini, stirring and tossing to coat in the emulsified sauce (if the sauce seems too thick to coat the noodles, stir in more water about a tablespoon at a time). Once the noodles are heated through, remove the pan from the heat.

Transfer the bucatini to a wide bowl or serving platter, spooning any sauce left in the pan on top. Sprinkle with whatever combination of chopped eggs, pork rinds, Parmesan, scallions, fried garlic, and/or black pepper you have on hand. Serve warm with lemon wedges, if desired, for squeezing over the top.

Tteokbokki all'Amatriciana

1 tablespoon extra-virgin olive oil, plus more as needed

6 ounces thick-cut bacon, pancetta, or guanciale, cut into ½-inch pieces

1 medium yellow onion, finely diced

1 teaspoon gochugaru (Korean chile flakes) or red chile flakes

Kosher salt and freshly ground black pepper

2 cloves garlic, minced

2 tablespoons tomato paste

1 (28-ounce) can crushed tomatoes

1 pound (or 500 grams) fresh or frozen cylinder-shaped rice cakes (tteok)

½ cup freshly grated Pecorino Romano or Parmesan cheese

Chopped parsley (optional), for serving

SERVES 4 TO 6

In a large saucepan, heat the olive oil and bacon over medium heat and cook, stirring often, until the fat is rendered and the bacon is crispy, 5 to 7 minutes. Using a slotted spoon, transfer the bacon to a small bowl, leaving the rendered fat behind in the skillet.

Add the onion, gochugaru, and a generous pinch of salt and pepper to the pan and cook over medium-low heat, stirring often, until the onions are soft and browned around the edges, 5 to 7 minutes. Add the garlic and cook, stirring constantly, until fragrant, 1 to 2 minutes.

Add the tomato paste and cook, stirring constantly so it doesn't scorch, until it thickens and darkens in color, 3 to 4 minutes. Stir in the crushed tomatoes and the reserved crispy pork, then reduce the heat to a simmer and cook for about 15 minutes to let the sauce thicken while you cook the tteok (rice cakes).

Fill a large nonstick skillet two-thirds full with water and a few pinches of salt and bring to a boil. Add the tteok and cook until tender according to the package directions (usually just a few minutes). Reserving ¼ cup of the starchy water, drain the tteok well and return to the skillet over medium-high heat.

Add a generous tablespoon or so of olive oil to coat the tteok, then stir-fry the rice cakes until they become crispy around the edges (don't worry if they stick to the pan a little), 3 to 4 minutes.

Reduce the heat to low. Pour the sauce into the skillet and toss to combine, adding half of the grated pecorino and a splash or two of the reserved starchy water as needed to help loosen the sauce. Toss until the sauce evenly coats the rice cakes. Sprinkle with the remaining pecorino and the parsley, if using. Serve hot.

I've been obsessed with pasta all'Amatriciana since my culinary school days. That's because, despite its fancy-sounding name, the core technique at work is using the rendered fat from cured pork (traditionally guanciale or pancetta, but you can also use thick-cut bacon) as a means to emulsify tomato sauce, which creates a rich tomato gravy bobbing with chunks of braised crispy pork. Of all the Italian meat sauces, it ranks highest on the flavor-to-effort ratio. It's traditionally served with chewier, denser pasta like bucatini or rigatoni, which would be delicious here, but I go one step further and use tteok, soft and chewy tube-shaped Korean rice cakes that are the perfect foil to the hearty sauce. They're usually sold in vacuum-sealed shelf-stable bags or in the frozen section at Asian supermarkets. Either kind will work here.

Mushroom & Krab Cream Udon

1 pound udon noodles, fresh or frozen

2 cups chopped fresh mushrooms (about 8 ounces total), such as shiitake and enoki

4 tablespoons (½ stick) butter

2 scallions, thinly sliced, white and green parts kept separate

4 cloves garlic, minced or grated

1 tablespoon shiro (white) miso

1 tablespoon oyster sauce

6 ounces imitation crabmeat, shredded

¾ cup heavy cream, half-and-half, or evaporated milk

½ teaspoon chicken bouillon powder, plus more to taste

¼ teaspoon ground white pepper, plus more to taste

Juice of ½ lemon

Furikake, for garnish

SERVES 4

If using frozen udon noodles, soak them in hot water for about 1 minute to loosen, then carefully separate the noodles. Rinse with cold water, drain, and set aside.

Heat a large dry skillet over medium-high heat. Once the pan is hot, add the mushrooms and cook, stirring occasionally, until the mushrooms give up their moisture and start to brown in the dry pan, 4 to 5 minutes.

Add the butter, scallion whites, garlic, miso, and oyster sauce. Cook, stirring, for 1 to 2 minutes, until a thick sauce forms (if the miso clumps, add a tablespoon or two of water to dissolve it).

Stir in the shredded crab and cream and bring to a simmer Add the udon and continue cooking, stirring and tossing often, until the sauce has thickened and the udon noodles are al dente, 2 to 3 minutes.

Season with the bouillon powder and white pepper, tasting and adding more as needed. Remove the pan from the heat and stir in the lemon juice. Garnish with the reserved scallion greens and furikake before serving warm.

Udon noodles and imitation crab are two items I always have in my freezer. Not only do they last forever, but their texture isn't harmed by the freezing process, they thaw quickly, and they're a solid foundation for a fast dinner. Pick up a mix of mushrooms on the way home, add fresh or frozen vegetables and seasoning staples like miso and chicken broth, and you're 20 minutes away from these creamy, umami-packed noodles made in one pan. Remember that the best way to sauté mushrooms is to sear them in a hot, dry pan. They'll give up the water trapped inside them and concentrate in flavor as they soften and brown.

Filipino Spaghetti Bake

Kosher salt

1 pound spaghetti

2 tablespoons extra-virgin olive oil

1 medium yellow onion, finely chopped

6 cloves garlic, minced

1 pound ground beef (80/20)

1 tablespoon fish sauce or shoyu (soy sauce)

2 teaspoons beef bouillon powder

1 teaspoon gochugaru (Korean chile flakes) or red chile flakes

1 teaspoon garlic powder

1 teaspoon Italian seasoning

1 teaspoon freshly ground black pepper

1 (29-ounce) can tomato sauce

1 (6-ounce) can tomato paste

10 hot dogs, cut diagonally into ¼-inch-thick slices

¼ cup sweetened condensed milk

¼ cup banana ketchup (see Note) or honey barbecue sauce

1 (10-ounce) can cream of mushroom soup

2 cups shredded Colby Jack cheese (or a mix of mozzarella or Jack cheese and mild Cheddar)

SERVES 8

Preheat the oven to 350°F.

In a large pot of boiling salted water, cook the spaghetti according to the package directions for al dente. Drain and set aside.

Meanwhile, in a large skillet, heat the olive oil over medium heat until shimmering. Add the onion and garlic and cook, stirring often, until fragrant, about a minute. Add the ground beef and cook, stirring often, until browned and broken up into small pieces, 6 to 8 minutes. (Drain off the excess fat now, if desired.)

Add the fish sauce, bouillon powder, gochugaru, garlic powder, Italian seasoning, and black pepper. Stir to combine. Add the tomato sauce, tomato paste, sliced hot dogs, sweetened condensed milk, and banana ketchup. Stir well and simmer, uncovered, for 10 to 15 minutes to let the sauce thicken and flavors combine.

Stir in the drained spaghetti and mix until the noodles are well coated with the sauce.

In an ungreased 9 × 13-inch baking dish, spread the cream of mushroom soup evenly along the bottom, then pour the spaghetti mixture over the mushroom soup layer. Top with the shredded cheese.

Bake uncovered until the cheese is melted and bubbling, 25 to 30 minutes. Serve warm.

When you need to feed a lot of hungry people, turn to this spaghetti bake. You might remember spaghetti bake from school lunch days. It was one of my favorites, up there with sheet pan pizza, fried chicken patties with gravy, and yellow peaches from the can.

The style of spaghetti in this recipe is distinct, though: It's a mashup of Filipino and American traditions, familiar to anyone who has had the similar version at the Filipino fast-food chain Jollibee. Imagine a sweeter, richer, more umami Bolognese sauce with sliced hot dogs and you've got a classic comfort food of the Philippines, made even more comforting here topped with shredded cheese and finished in the oven until bubbling.

Note: Filipino banana ketchup is a sweeter, less tangy style of ketchup made with pureed bananas. If you can't find it, the closest substitute is not actually regular ketchup, but your favorite sweet barbecue sauce. Seems like a minor detail, but it does make a difference in taste.

“Dan Dan” Instant Noodles

For the dan dan sauce

1 tablespoon neutral oil, plus more for storing

½ pound ground pork

2 tablespoons finely chopped bread-and-butter pickles

3 tablespoons shoyu (soy sauce)

2 teaspoons chicken bouillon powder

¼ teaspoon ground white pepper

¼ cup extra-crunchy peanut butter

3 cloves garlic, minced or grated

2 teaspoons light brown sugar

2 teaspoons rice vinegar

1 teaspoon Worcestershire sauce

Toasted sesame oil (optional), as needed

For serving

2 (3-ounce) packages instant noodles, flavor packets saved for another use

3 scallions, thinly sliced, for garnish

Chili crisp, for serving

SERVES 2

Make the dan dan sauce: In a skillet, heat the neutral oil over high heat until shimmering. Add the ground pork and cook, breaking up with a spatula, until lightly browned, 3 to 4 minutes. Stir in the chopped pickles, 1 tablespoon of the shoyu, the bouillon powder, and white pepper. Cook, scraping up any browned bits, until the liquid evaporates and the pork begins to brown again, about 1 minute. Add the remaining 2 tablespoons shoyu, the peanut butter, garlic, brown sugar, rice vinegar, and Worcestershire sauce. Stir until combined, then remove the pan from the heat and transfer the dan dan sauce to a lidded jar. Drizzle a small amount of sesame oil, if using, or neutral oil to form a thin layer over the sauce, then place in the fridge until ready to use (up to 5 days).

When you're ready to serve: Cook the instant noodles according to the package directions. Drain off most of the hot starchy noodle water into a heatproof jar or cup (it's fine if there's a little at the bottom of the pot). Stir in the dan dan sauce, adding some of the hot water back as needed until a loose, smooth sauce forms that coats the noodles. Top with the scallions and as much chili crisp as desired.

If you're on social media as much as my kids, you probably know there's plenty of viral recipes on how to make instant noodles fancy. This is my contribution to the genre: bootleg dan dan noodles that you can prepare in advance and store in the fridge for several days until you're ready to eat. Add the concentrated dan dan mixture to drained hot noodles, and the residual water at the bottom will emulsify the paste into a thick noodle-clinging sauce. If you're iffy about cooking the pork and freezing it, firm tofu is a great substitute (see Note). I also use sweet chopped pickles in lieu of pickled Chinese mustard greens, and a combination of rice vinegar and Worcestershire as a stand-in for Chinese black vinegar.

Any type of dried noodle will work here, as well as the udon or yakisoba noodles you'll find in the refrigerated section at grocery stores. And while I like my dan dan noodles spicy, I serve this with chili crisp on the side, so everyone can adjust it to their desired heat level.

This recipe only makes enough dan dan sauce for two standard packages of instant noodles, but if you want to really be efficient, you can scale up the sauce to taste, portion it into individual containers, and freeze it. That way, the next time you boil noodles, all you'll need to do is thaw and mix for a quick meal.

Note: To make the dish vegan, omit the pork and substitute with extra-firm tofu, pressed dry and then crumbled. And use mushroom bouillon powder instead of chicken and balsamic vinegar in place of Worcestershire sauce (or vegan Worcestershire sauce).

Lox & Schmear Onigiri

- 8 ounces cream cheese
- ¼ cup sugar, plus more to taste
- 2 tablespoons kosher salt, plus more to taste
- 8 ounces salmon fillet, skinned and pin bones removed
- 2 cups short-grain rice (or 6 cups cooked rice)
- 3 tablespoons everything bagel seasoning
- 2 tablespoons finely chopped fresh chives
- 8 shiso leaves, torn in half, or ¼ cup dill fronds (optional)
- 8 snack-size nori sheets

MAKES 8

Place the block of cream cheese in the freezer to firm up while you cure the salmon, 20 to 30 minutes (this will make the cream cheese easier to cube).

In a small bowl, mix together the sugar and salt to make a cure. Holding the knife at a forty-five-degree angle to the cutting board, thinly slice the salmon fillet into about ¼-inch-thick slices. Sprinkle half of the cure across a large dinner plate or small sheet pan, then arrange the slices in a single layer over the top. Sprinkle on the remaining cure, making sure the salmon is completely covered. Cover tightly with plastic wrap and press down firmly. Place in the fridge for 1 hour.

Meanwhile, if you haven't already, cook the rice using a rice cooker according to the manufacturer's instructions. Once finished, turn off the rice cooker and keep the lid closed rather than use the "keep warm" setting.

Once the cream cheese is firm (but not frozen solid), remove from the freezer and cut into 8 slices, then halve each of those slices so you have 16 squares. Transfer to a bowl and return to the freezer.

Once the salmon is finished curing, rinse the cure off the slices in a colander and pat them dry with a paper towel. Cut each slice into four equal-size chunks and set aside.

In a large bowl, combine the cooked rice, 2 tablespoons of the bagel seasoning, and the chives and stir until evenly mixed. Since the amount of salt can be different depending on the bagel seasoning brand, taste and adjust with salt and sugar as needed. Remove the cream cheese slices from the freezer.

recipe continues →

Who needs a bagel when you have onigiri? Salmon-filled rice balls are a classic snack in Hawai'i, and these take it to the next level by quick-curing your own salmon in salt and sugar, and stuffing the warm rice with nuggets of chilled cream cheese that become smooth and creamy as they soften. A sprinkle of everything seasoning stands in for furikake. Making your own lox is worth the surprisingly low amount of effort required, but if you want to skip that step, sliced smoked salmon will also work.

Wet your hands lightly with water to prevent the rice from sticking when you make the onigiri. Take a large handful of cooked rice (about ¾ cup) and gently flatten it in your palm until it's about the size of a compact disc. Place 2 pieces of cream cheese, a few pieces of shiso or dill (if using), and about a tablespoon's worth of salmon into the center, then gently fold the rice over the filling to enclose it, shaping it into a triangular or egg shape (you can also use an onigiri mold for this step). Press firmly to compact together.

Repeat the process until all the rice is used, making about 8 onigiri. Wrap a sheet of nori around the base of each, then sprinkle them with the remaining 1 tablespoon bagel seasoning, pressing it gently onto the surface of the rice to adhere. Serve immediately.

Matthew Fober (right) and Amy Geisler, owners of Pauwela Produce, supply our restaurants with microgreens and vegetables.

Chicken Adobo Fried Rice

3 tablespoons neutral oil

4 large eggs, lightly beaten

Kosher salt

8 cloves garlic, chopped

1 bay leaf

1 pound boneless, skinless chicken thighs, cut into ½-inch pieces

½ cup plus 2 tablespoons apple cider vinegar

1 tablespoon oyster sauce

2 tablespoons shoyu (soy sauce)

Freshly ground black pepper

4 cups chilled cooked rice (preferably refrigerated overnight)

1 teaspoon sugar

½ cup thinly sliced scallions

SERVES 4

In a large skillet, heat 1 tablespoon of the oil over medium-high heat until shimmering. Pour in the eggs and season with a pinch of salt. Cook, stirring constantly, until softly scrambled and just set, about 2 minutes. Transfer the eggs to a plate and set aside.

Wipe out any bits of egg from the pan, return to the heat, and heat the remaining 2 tablespoons oil until shimmering. Add the garlic and bay leaf and cook, stirring frequently, until the garlic is fragrant and begins to soften, less than 1 minute. Add the chicken and stir-fry until the chicken is browned in spots, about 1 minute. Add the ½ cup vinegar, the oyster sauce, 1 tablespoon of the shoyu, and ½ teaspoon black pepper. Cook for another 2 to 3 minutes, stirring often, until the chicken is cooked through and has absorbed most of the sauce. Discard the bay leaf.

Add the rice to the pan, tossing with the saucy chicken and making sure any clumps of rice are broken up. Stir in the reserved scrambled eggs and the sugar. Once the fried rice is heated through, stir in the remaining 2 tablespoons vinegar, the remaining 1 tablespoon shoyu, and a pinch of salt and pepper. Once the rice has absorbed the liquid, stir in the scallions and remove the pan from the heat. Serve immediately.

Adobo fried rice is usually made with leftover adobo, which tends to be something of a regular occurrence in Filipino households where the dish is cooked in big batches (I've got the Tupperware stains to prove it). But if you find yourself with a specific craving for adobo fried rice like I sometimes do, this creates something of a chicken-and-egg problem. Do I need to cook a whole portion of adobo so I can have leftovers to make fried rice with? The answer is heck no.

Most kinds of adobo are made by simmering some kind of protein in a mix of shoyu, vinegar, and spices. In this case, however, I'm stir-frying chicken thighs in the same seasonings so they soak up the flavor, which forms the basis for the fried rice. I didn't make this clear enough in the fried rice recipe from my first cookbook, but one element I can't stress enough is: There's no such thing as too many scallions in fried rice. So don't skimp. More green is always more better.

Okinawan Taco Rice page 118

Okinawan Taco Rice

For the pico de gallo

½ medium white onion, finely chopped (save the other half for the taco meat)

2 plum tomatoes, finely chopped

1 jalapeño, seeded and finely chopped

¼ cup chopped fresh cilantro leaves

1 tablespoon fresh lime juice

Kosher salt

For the taco meat

2 tablespoons neutral oil

½ medium white onion, finely chopped

1 pound ground beef (80/20)

3 cloves garlic, minced or grated

3 tablespoons tomato paste

2 tablespoons shoyu (soy sauce)

2 tablespoons chili powder

1 tablespoon rice vinegar

2 teaspoons ground cumin

1 teaspoon gochugaru (Korean chile flakes) or red chile flakes

1 teaspoon dried oregano

1 teaspoon paprika

1 teaspoon sugar

Kosher salt and freshly ground black pepper

Make the pico de gallo: In a medium bowl, combine the onion, tomatoes, jalapeño, cilantro, lime juice, and a few pinches of salt. Mix thoroughly. Taste and season with more salt as needed. Refrigerate until ready to serve.

Make the taco meat: In a large skillet, heat the oil over medium-high heat until shimmering. Add the onion and cook, stirring often, until softened and fragrant, 2 to 3 minutes. Add the ground beef and garlic and cook, breaking it apart with a spatula, until the meat is browned and cooked through, 5 to 7 minutes.

Stir in the tomato paste, shoyu, chili powder, vinegar, cumin, gochugaru, oregano, paprika, sugar, and ¼ cup water. Stir well to combine, season with a big pinch of salt and pepper, then simmer for 5 minutes until the sauce has thickened. Taste and season with more salt and pepper as needed. Remove the pan from the heat.

To assemble: In a small bowl, mix together the sour cream and mayo until combined. Stir in a tablespoon of water, or more as needed, until it can be easily drizzled. Divide the cooked rice among four shallow bowls. Top each with equal portions of crushed corn chips, taco meat, shredded cheese, lettuce, pico de gallo, and the sour cream mixture. Serve immediately with your favorite taco sauce and lime wedges.

Okinawan taco rice is a unique mashup of the Mexican-American ground beef taco—the kind with crunchy shells, shredded lettuce, and grated yellow cheese—and Japanese rice bowls. A restaurant in Okinawa invented the dish in the 1980s, and it's become a cultural phenomenon. Thinking goes that it was invented due to US servicemen craving Mexican food while being stationed on Okinawa, but it also speaks to the creativity and ingenuity Okinawan cooks are known for, a reputation that also stands here in Hawaiʻi, where a good chunk of the Japanese community is Okinawan. More to the point though, taco rice is as tasty as it is quick to prepare. Swap out tortillas for rice next Taco Tuesday and you won't be disappointed.

For assembly

¾ cup sour cream

¼ cup mayonnaise

6 cups cooked short-grain rice

1½ cups lightly crushed Fritos or other corn chips

1½ cups finely shredded Mexican cheese blend

1½ cups shredded iceberg lettuce (about ½ head)

Your favorite taco sauce, for serving

Lime wedges, for squeezing

SERVES 4

Friends Sadie and Donovan—an artisan sourdough baker—with their son

Lap Cheong Red Beans & Rice

- 3 tablespoons salted butter
- 1 medium yellow onion, finely diced
- 1 medium green bell pepper, finely diced
- 2 stalks celery, finely diced
- 1 clove garlic, minced
- 8 ounces lap cheong sausage (about 6 links), sliced into ¼-inch coins
- 1 (15-ounce) can red kidney beans, rinsed and drained
- 1¾ cups low-sodium chicken broth
- 2 teaspoons Cajun or Creole seasoning, plus more to taste
- 1 cup long-grain rice
- 2 scallions, thinly sliced, for garnish

SERVES 4 TO 6

In a large skillet with a lid or a Dutch oven, melt the butter over medium heat. Once the foam has subsided, add the onion, bell pepper, celery, and garlic. Cook, stirring occasionally, until the vegetables are softened, 5 to 7 minutes.

Scrape the cooked vegetables into a small bowl and set aside. Add the sliced sausages to the skillet and cook, stirring occasionally, until browned all over, 5 to 6 minutes.

Return the sautéed vegetables to the skillet and add the kidney beans, chicken broth, and Cajun seasoning. Stir to combine. Stir in the uncooked rice, making sure the grains are evenly distributed. Bring the mixture to a boil. Reduce the heat to low, cover, and simmer, stirring occasionally to prevent sticking, until the rice is cooked and almost all of the liquid is absorbed, 20 to 25 minutes.

Remove the skillet from the heat and garnish with the scallions before serving.

It's always a good idea to have a package of lap cheong in your cupboard. You'll find this sweet, dry-cured style of sausage at any decent-size Chinese market, sealed in shelf-stable packaging that keeps it usable for months, maybe even years. As kids, it was one of our favorite snacks to bring on camping trips, and if we couldn't get our hands on some, we'd improvise the flavor by dipping pepperoni sticks in sugar (not recommended unless you're desperate). A classic way to use lap cheong is to cook the sausage in a pot of rice, softening the cured links as they add flavor to the rice while it cooks.

At some point I had the idea of pushing that concept one step further by adding lap cheong to one of my favorite Southern home-cooking dishes, red beans and rice. This one-pot meal combines the Creole holy trinity of onion, bell pepper, and celery with smoky-sweet lap cheong and a few shakes of seasoning (I like Tony Chachere's Creole seasoning) to elevate its two starchy core elements. Make sure not to skip the step of slowly browning the sliced sausage: As the fat renders from the pork, it mixes with the sugar in the lap cheong to create a sticky, snappy crust that contrasts nicely with the soft-cooked beans and rice.

Triple-Garlic Rice

- 3 tablespoons neutral oil
- 8 cloves garlic, minced
- 4 cups cooked rice, cooled
- ½ teaspoon kosher salt, plus more to taste
- ½ teaspoon sugar, plus more to taste
- ½ teaspoon garlic powder, or to taste
- ½ teaspoon MSG (optional)
- ½ teaspoon ground white pepper
- Scallions, finely chopped, for garnish
- Fried Garlic (page 30) or store-bought, for garnish

SERVES 4

In a 12-inch skillet or wok, heat the oil over medium-low heat until shimmering. Add the garlic and cook, stirring very often, until it turns a deep golden color (but not brown), 2 to 3 minutes.

Add the cooked rice, breaking up any clumps with a spatula or spoon. Increase the heat to medium-high and sprinkle in the salt, sugar, garlic powder, MSG (if using), and white pepper, stirring well to combine. Continue to stir-fry the rice for a few minutes until it's heated through and glistening. Taste and adjust the seasoning as needed.

Transfer to a serving dish, garnish with the scallions and fried garlic, and serve warm.

With garlic rice, it's all there in the name. This minimalist fried rice is more than satisfying on its own, but not so overpowering that it can't be a background singer for other main dishes (it's a must-have with Pork Belly Tocino, page 56, for Filipino breakfast, for me).

This version is what I would call the garlic lover's garlic fried rice, in that fresh garlic is still at the forefront, but there are several other garlicky elements that deepen its flavor, including garlic powder, which adds a distinct mellow, rounder garlic flavor, and fried garlic, which adds a crunchy contrast.

As with most fried rice, I recommend using day-old leftover rice here. That said, since the additional ingredients for garlic rice are minimal, you can definitely get away with using freshly cooked rice that's been cooled to room temperature.

Scallion Rice

2 tablespoons neutral oil

10 scallions, thinly sliced, white and green parts kept separate

½ teaspoon kosher salt, plus more to taste

3 cups freshly cooked rice, warm

SERVES 3 OR 4

In a small skillet, heat the oil over medium heat until shimmering. Add the scallion whites and sprinkle with the salt. Cook, stirring, for about 1 minute, until the whites have softened and become fragrant.

Scrape the scallion whites and oil from the pan into the rice and stir to combine. Add the scallion greens, then stir to combine again. Taste and season with more salt as needed; the rice should taste balanced but not strongly seasoned.

Serve immediately.

If you've gotten this far in the book, you might have noticed that I love putting scallions over everything. They add freshness, fragrance, and flavor, and there really is no such thing as using too many. A handful of scallions over a dish is great, but a more robust way to incorporate that bright, oniony taste is to cook this basic rice infused with huge wafts of scallion-ness.

The key is to separate the green and white parts of the scallions: The whites are briefly stir-fried in oil to soften and sweeten their pungency, and then finely sliced greens give the rice a pop of emerald color and that wonderful allium aroma. Unlike fried rice, freshly cooked rice works better than refrigerated leftover rice in this situation. It's fantastic eaten with something as minimal as a fried egg, but I also like swapping it in with dishes you might normally serve with plain rice—including Shoyu Chicken (page 151), Oven Galbijjim (page 219), and Bistek Bites (page 191).

Toasted Coconut Grits

½ cup grits, preferably stone-ground

¼ cup unsweetened coconut flakes (optional)

1 (13-ounce) can full-fat coconut milk

Kosher salt

2 tablespoons butter or extra-virgin olive oil (optional)

Freshly ground black pepper

SERVES 4

In a medium saucepan or Dutch oven, toast the grits and coconut flakes (if using) over medium-low heat, stirring often, until the grits develop a light brown color (the coconut will toast a bit faster), 5 to 7 minutes.

While stirring, slowly pour in the coconut milk and 2½ cups water and add a few big pinches of salt. Increase the heat to bring to a boil, then reduce to a simmer. Cover and cook at a simmer, stirring occasionally and adding more water as needed if the mixture seems too thick, until the grits are creamy and tender, 45 minutes to 1 hour.

Stir in the butter (if using) and season with pepper and more salt to taste. Serve warm.

Aunty Pi'ilani, a pillar in the upcountry farmers market and Maui community

Rice is the go-to starch in much of this book, but I do love some creamy Southern-style grits, too. These have a bit of a Caribbean element to them with the addition of coconut in two ways: nutty coconut flakes that get pan-toasted along with the grits (always toast your grits for flavor!) and creamy coconut milk mixed into the cooking liquid. These grits are delicious on their own, but they're the perfect partner for Beef Pares (page 216) or any other saucy braised dishes.

177

SOUPS & STEWS

Japanese Corn Egg Drop

- 2 cups low-sodium or unsalted chicken broth
- 1 (15-ounce) can no-salt-added or regular whole sweet kernel corn, with its liquid
- 1 teaspoon shoyu (soy sauce)
- ½ teaspoon HonDashi powder or 1 teaspoon shiro (white) miso (or both)
- 2 teaspoons potato starch or cornstarch
- 1 large egg
- 1 tablespoon unsalted butter
- Kosher salt
- 3 tablespoons thinly sliced scallions, green parts only
- Ground white pepper

SERVES 2

In a medium saucepan, combine the chicken broth, corn and liquid, shoyu, and HonDashi and bring to a boil over medium-high heat.

Meanwhile, in a small bowl, whisk the potato starch with 1 tablespoon water until it dissolves into a slurry.

Once the soup is boiling, reduce the heat until the liquid is at a bare simmer. While stirring, pour in the slurry and continue stirring until the starch is fully combined and the soup has thickened slightly, about a minute.

Crack the egg into a small bowl or measuring cup and beat well with a chopstick. Then, using the chopstick as a guide, pour the beaten egg into the soup by drizzling it from the bowl down the chopstick in a thin stream. You'll want to pour the egg into the soup in a circular motion so it doesn't end up in just one part of the pot.

Remove the pot from the heat to keep the egg from overcooking and add the butter. Once the butter is melted, gently stir to combine. Taste and season with a pinch of salt, if needed.

Divide the soup into bowls and sprinkle with the scallion greens and a dash of white pepper before serving.

One busy school morning, I cobbled this soup together and packed it in Thermoses for my kids' lunches. It had elements of several soups that I love—corn chowder, egg drop soup, a little miso soup thrown in—but it wasn't quite any of them. When the kids came home, they immediately wanted to know what it was, and when was I going to make it again, which is proof enough that you've got a hit on your hands.

The secret here is to use the liquid that comes in a can of corn as part of the broth. Yes, canned corn. It adds a distinct sweet, savory corn essence to the soup that you can't replicate otherwise. Simple but also very nourishing, this concoction is well suited for breakfast on a cold day, or when you're sick and don't want to exert too much effort. Try to use low-sodium or unsalted chicken broth and a can of no-salt-added corn so that you can adjust the seasoning levels yourself, but if you can only find one or the other, that will work fine, too.

Takeout Hot & Sour

- 1 tablespoon neutral oil
- 1 tablespoon grated fresh ginger
- 3 scallions, thinly sliced, white and green parts kept separate
- 8 ounces fresh shiitake or baby bella mushrooms, thinly sliced
- ¼ to ½ pound chicken, pork, or shrimp (optional), cut into bite-size pieces
- 4 cups low-sodium chicken broth
- ⅓ cup rice vinegar, plus more to taste
- 3 tablespoons shoyu (soy sauce)
- 3 tablespoons cornstarch
- 1 tablespoon toasted sesame oil
- 2 teaspoons chili garlic sauce or sambal oelek, plus more to taste
- 1 teaspoon Worcestershire sauce
- ¼ teaspoon ground white pepper, plus more to taste
- 1 (14-ounce) block firm tofu, drained, patted dry, and cut into thin batons
- Kosher salt or chicken bouillon powder
- 2 large eggs, lightly beaten

SERVES 4 TO 6

In a medium pot, heat the neutral oil over medium-high heat until shimmering. Add the ginger and scallion whites and cook for about a minute, stirring, until fragrant.

Add the mushrooms and whatever meat you're using, if any, and cook until the mushrooms are softened and the protein is cooked through—the timing will depend on the meat (if you're using shrimp, hold off on adding it until the mushrooms are softened). Add the chicken broth and increase the heat to bring to a boil.

Meanwhile, in a small bowl, whisk together the vinegar, shoyu, cornstarch, sesame oil, chili garlic sauce, Worcestershire sauce, and white pepper.

Pour into the boiling broth while stirring, then reduce the heat to a simmer and cook until the soup has thickened, 4 to 5 minutes. Stir in the tofu and cook until heated through, another 1 to 2 minutes. Taste and season with more vinegar and white pepper as needed, and add salt to taste. If you like your hot and sour hotter, you can add more chili garlic sauce, too.

Remove the pot from the heat and slowly drizzle in the beaten eggs while stirring constantly to form scrambled egg ribbons. Stir in the reserved scallion greens and serve hot.

My favorite recipes are what the Japanese call *nabemono,* or one-pot dishes. This streamlined take on the tangy and savory Chinese restaurant staple isn't Japanese, of course, but it is a great example of a satisfying, flavorful soup that can be pulled together in about 30 minutes on a rainy weeknight while your kids are watching an episode of *Paw Patrol*. And it can all be done in one pot, no less. Great for using up any odds and ends of meat left in the fridge, too.

Sinigang Verde

1 pound boneless pork shoulder, cut into ¾-inch pieces

For the green sauce

1 large poblano pepper, stemmed, seeded, and chopped

2 large jalapeños, stemmed, seeded, and chopped

1 bunch of scallions, chopped, green and white parts kept separate

4 cloves garlic, smashed and peeled

1 teaspoon coriander seeds

1 teaspoon cumin seeds

4 medium tomatillos, roughly chopped

2 tablespoons fish sauce

½ bunch of cilantro

½ cup distilled white vinegar

In a large pot or Dutch oven, cook the pork shoulder over high heat, turning every minute or so, until the meat is browned on all sides, 6 to 8 minutes. Transfer the browned pork to a plate and set aside, leaving any rendered fat in the pot.

Make the green sauce: Reduce the heat to medium-high. To the same pot, add the poblanos, jalapeños, scallion whites, garlic, coriander seeds, and cumin seeds. Cook, stirring occasionally, until the vegetables are tender, 3 to 4 minutes.

Add the chopped tomatillos and fish sauce and cook until the tomatillos soften and give up their liquid, another 3 to 4 minutes.

Remove from the heat and carefully transfer the tomatillo mixture to a blender. Add the cilantro, reserved scallion greens, vinegar, and 1 cup water. Blend until smooth and set the green sauce aside.

recipe and ingredients continue →

This vegetable-rich stew started out as a fun, off-the-cuff special for Tin Roof, which happens to be directly across the parking lot from a Mexican restaurant. The thinking was, what if we combined Filipino sinigang with Mexican chile verde? Sinigang is traditionally accented with sour ingredients like citrus or tamarind, and chile verde brings the tartness with green tomatillos. As it turned out, we had stumbled onto a crossover that made a surprising amount of sense for cooking at home.

When most of us think about making a soup or stew, our minds go to putting everything in a pot at once and cooking them together until done, which can be great in something like chili or pot roast but usually produces a dish that's fairly homogeneous. Here we're cooking different layers of the stew at different times and at high intensities, and sometimes not cooking them at all, which creates contrasting flavors and textures that keeps each bite interesting and saves a lot of simmering time, too.

After browning chunks of pork, this recipe starts with a flavorful base made from cooked-down aromatics and tomatillos, which then gets blended with fresh herbs and vinegar to create a bright and vibrant green sauce. The browned pork and vegetables are then simmered in broth to make a basic soup, with the green sauce added at the final minute to punch things up. What you end up with is a one-pot meal that doesn't take all day to cook but has a serious depth of flavor and complexity to it. Spicy, tangy, rich, and savory, this version of sinigang has become a favorite for family meals at the restaurants, and is also a big hit for weeknight dinners.

For the sinigang broth

6 cups chicken broth

2-inch piece fresh ginger, finely julienned

1 firm Roma tomato, cut into wedges

½ medium yellow onion, cut into wedges

½ pound green beans, trimmed and cut into 1-inch pieces

½ pound okra (frozen or fresh), trimmed and cut into 1-inch pieces

½ pound shishito peppers, trimmed and cut into 1-inch pieces

Kosher salt and freshly ground black pepper

For serving

1 cup fresh watercress, roughly chopped

1 cup lightly crushed chicharrones and/or corn nuts

Cooked white rice

Chile Vinegar (page 261)

SERVES 8

Make the sinigang broth: To the same pot, return the pork and add the chicken broth, ginger, tomato, and onion. Bring to a boil, then reduce the heat to medium-low and simmer, covered, until the pork shoulder is tender, about 20 minutes.

Stir in the green beans, okra, and shishito peppers and bring to a boil. Then remove the pot from the heat. Stir in the green sauce. Season with salt and black pepper to taste.

To serve: Serve the soup hot, topped with watercress and crushed chicharrones and/or corn nuts, with cooked rice and chile vinegar on the side.

I learned some amazing recipes from my Uncle Danny. Here he is with my cousin Desiree and my niece Sloan.

Curried Mung Beans

2 tablespoons extra-virgin olive oil, plus more for serving

½ large yellow onion, finely chopped

1 tablespoon minced fresh ginger

2 cloves garlic, minced

1 medium tomato, diced

1 teaspoon Thai red curry paste, plus more to taste

2 cups low-sodium broth (chicken or vegetable) or water

1 cup canned full-fat coconut milk

2 tablespoons fish sauce or shoyu (soy sauce), plus more to taste

1 tablespoon brown sugar, plus more to taste

1 serrano chile or jalapeño, seeded and finely chopped

1 cup split mung beans or lentils, rinsed

4 ounces green beans, trimmed and cut into 1-inch pieces (about 1 cup)

1 cup packed spinach leaves

Handful of basil leaves (optional), for serving

Lime wedges (optional), for serving

SERVES 6

In a large pot or Dutch oven, heat the olive oil over medium heat until shimmering. Add the onion, ginger, and garlic and sauté until fragrant and softened, 1 to 2 minutes. Stir in the tomato and curry paste and cook, stirring frequently, until the flavors are released and some of the liquid from the tomato has cooked off, another 1 to 2 minutes.

Stir in the broth, coconut milk, fish sauce, brown sugar, and chile. Taste and stir in more curry paste if desired. Add the mung beans to the pot, then increase the heat and bring to a boil. Once boiling, reduce the heat to a simmer, cover, and cook, stirring occasionally, until the mung beans are tender, 20 to 25 minutes.

Add the green beans and cook until crisp-tender, 4 to 6 minutes.

Add the spinach and cook until tender, about a minute. Taste and adjust the seasoning with fish sauce or sugar.

Serve warm, garnished with basil leaves and lime wedges on the side, if you like.

If my older brother, Jeremy, had a death-row meal, I'm sure it would be balatong, an Ilocano dish from the Philippines that's more or less mung beans cooked down with greens and bits of pork belly until it yields a rich, hearty stew. Remove the pork belly from the equation and you've got a fantastic plant-centric one-pot meal that comes together quickly. But, of course, as Filipinos know, pork belly provides flavor, so my approach here is to plug in the bold seasonings of Southeast Asian curry in its place, which fits with the rest of the ingredients like a glove. This recipe is flexible in that with "beans and greens" as a base, you can add or remove vegetables according to what you have on hand, or swap out the fish sauce for shoyu to make it vegetarian. Store-bought curry pastes can often vary in terms of potency and heat, so I like starting with a small amount and adjusting with more later as needed.

Bulalo

2½ pounds beef shank

½ large yellow onion, roughly chopped

1 large tomato, roughly chopped

2 stalks lemongrass, trimmed and smashed

3 bay leaves

3 cloves garlic, smashed and peeled

2-inch piece fresh ginger, sliced

3 tablespoons fish sauce

2 teaspoons black peppercorns

2 teaspoons kosher salt, plus more to taste

2 ears corn, shucked and cut into thirds

½ small head green cabbage, cored and leaves separated

2 tablespoons apple cider vinegar

Chile Vinegar (page 261), for serving

SERVES 6 TO 8

In a large pot, combine the beef shank with water to cover. Bring to a rolling boil, then remove the pot from the heat and dump out the water.

Rinse the shanks and return them to the pot. Add 8 cups water to the pot, plus the onion, tomato, lemongrass, bay leaves, garlic, ginger, 1 tablespoon of the fish sauce, the peppercorns, and salt. Bring to a boil. Reduce the heat to a simmer, partially cover, and cook at a simmer until the beef is tender, about 2 hours. (Alternatively, add all the ingredients to a pressure cooker and cook for 30 minutes at high pressure.)

Uncover, add the corn, and continue simmering, uncovered, until the corn is tender, about 10 minutes.

Remove the bay leaves and lemongrass, add the cabbage, the remaining 2 tablespoons fish sauce, the apple cider vinegar, and salt to taste. Continue simmering until the cabbage is tender, another 3 to 4 minutes.

Serve hot with chile vinegar on the side.

It speaks to the diversity of the Philippines that among my Filipino friends in Hawai'i, many of us grew up eating dishes that the other had never tried, or ever heard about, all because our parents or grandparents emigrated from different parts of the country. Occasionally, I would try one so delicious, I was mad I'd been missing out on it all that time. That was the case with bulalo, a clear beef shank soup that's one of my favorite things to eat on a quiet Sunday morning at home (I love a brothy breakfast). Bulalo is extremely simple, and all of its magic lies in its long-simmered broth. Using beef shanks is essential, since the connective bits and bone marrow contribute collagen and fat that make for a rich and flavorful soup.

Chili & Wieners

- 1 tablespoon neutral oil
- 1 medium sweet onion, finely diced
- 1 green bell pepper, finely diced
- 2 stalks celery, finely diced
- 3 cloves garlic, minced
- 1 pound ground beef (80/20)
- 8 ounces mild or hot linguiça (sometimes labeled Portuguese sausage), diced
- 1 tablespoon chili powder
- 2 teaspoons chicken bouillon powder
- 2 teaspoons light brown sugar
- 1 teaspoon ground cumin
- 1 teaspoon garlic powder
- 1 teaspoon smoked paprika
- 1 teaspoon gochugaru (Korean chile flakes) or red chile flakes
- 1 teaspoon Worcestershire sauce
- 1 (15-ounce) can crushed tomatoes
- 1 (15-ounce) can tomato sauce
- 1 (15-ounce) can pinto beans
- 1 (15-ounce) can red kidney beans
- 2 tablespoons mayonnaise
- 2 bay leaves

For serving

- 6 to 8 red franks, or your favorite hot dog
- Kosher salt and freshly ground black pepper
- Cooked rice
- Macaroni or potato salad, store-bought or homemade (see Note)
- Tabasco sauce

SERVES 6 TO 8

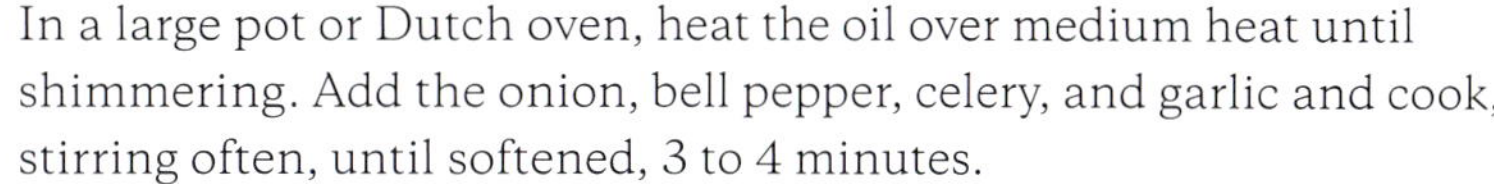

In a large pot or Dutch oven, heat the oil over medium heat until shimmering. Add the onion, bell pepper, celery, and garlic and cook, stirring often, until softened, 3 to 4 minutes.

Add the ground beef and linguiça to the pot, breaking up the beef into pieces and cooking until browned, 4 to 5 minutes. Stir in the chili powder, bouillon powder, brown sugar, cumin, garlic powder, smoked paprika, gochugaru, and Worcestershire sauce. Mix well to combine.

Add the crushed tomatoes, tomato sauce, and both canned beans *with their liquid* to the pot. Bring to a boil, then reduce the heat to a simmer and stir in the mayo and bay leaves. Loosely cover the pot and continue simmering, stirring occasionally, for about 30 minutes to allow the flavors to meld together.

Meanwhile, get ready to serve: Pan-fry, grill, or steam the franks until heated through (if pan-frying or grilling, score the casing of the hot dogs with a knife).

Discard the bay leaves and season the chili with salt and pepper to taste. Serve each bowl of chili with a wiener, rice, and potato or mac salad on top. Douse with Tabasco.

My brother, Jeremy, and I spent a lot of time on sports fields in high school—he was on the field or watching the game, and I was by the snack shack eating chili. Hawaiʻi takes a lot of pride in local-style chili and after many years of rigorous research, I've concluded the ultimate way to serve chili is with a wiener or two (ideally in the red casing) plus scoops of white rice and mac salad on top. Add a heavy shake of Tabasco and you've got what I call a balanced plate.

Note: Or go with my recipe for Mac Salad, which combines macaroni and potatoes. You can find it online at *Food & Wine* or in my first cookbook, *Cook Real Hawaiʻi*.

Uncle Danny's Tripe Stew

- 1 good-sized smoked pork hock (about ¾ pound)
- 4 cups low-sodium chicken stock
- 2 pounds honeycomb tripe
- 2 tablespoons neutral oil
- 6 cloves garlic, minced
- 1 tablespoon minced fresh ginger
- 1 tablespoon finely chopped celery leaves
- 1 large stalk celery, halved lengthwise and chopped
- 1 medium carrot, halved lengthwise and chopped
- ½ large green bell pepper, diced
- ½ large yellow onion, diced
- 1 (6-ounce) can tomato paste
- 1 (1.41-ounce) packet sazón seasoning
- 1 tablespoon shoyu (soy sauce)
- 1 teaspoon Maggi sauce
- Kosher salt and freshly ground black pepper
- ¼ cup finely chopped fresh cilantro leaves and stems
- Cooked white rice or sliced crusty bread, for serving

SERVES 6

In a large pot or Dutch oven, combine the pork hock and chicken stock and add enough water to cover the hock. Bring to a boil. Reduce to a gentle simmer, partially cover, and cook until the pork hock starts to fall apart when poked with a spoon, 2 to 3 hours. (The hock can also be cooked in a pressure cooker at high pressure for 30 minutes, or until tender.)

Transfer the hock to a plate to cool and pour the broth into a separate large container (the liquid will have reduced slightly).

Add the tripe to the pot and cover with cold water. Bring to a boil over high heat, then transfer the tripe to the plate to cool and dump out the water.

Once the hock and tripe are cool enough to handle, pick all the meat from the hock and give it a chop. Trim off any excess fat from the tripe and cut into short, bite-size strips.

Place the same large pot over medium-high heat, add the oil, and heat until shimmering. Add the garlic, ginger, and celery leaves and cook, stirring frequently, until fragrant, about 1 minute. Add the hock meat and tripe. Continue cooking, stirring constantly, until the moisture evaporates and the meat starts to stick to the sides of the pot, about 5 minutes.

Add the celery, carrot, bell pepper, and onion and continue cooking, stirring occasionally, until the vegetables begin to soften, another 5 minutes or so.

Stir in the reserved broth, the tomato paste, sazón, shoyu, and Maggi. Season to taste with salt and pepper. Reduce the heat to a simmer, partially cover, and simmer until the tripe is tender, 2 to 3 hours depending on your preference. Season to taste with salt and pepper. Remove from the heat and stir in the cilantro.

Serve warm with rice or crusty bread.

This stew is inspired by my Uncle Danny—and I mean my real uncle, since we call our elders "uncle" in Hawai'i out of respect—who for many years worked at Ken's House of Pancakes in Hilo, which, aside from great pancakes, was also famous for serving a mean tripe stew. He was a real cook's cook and a fixture at big family cookouts, especially if it involved making something old-school Ilocano, which usually meant some combination of offal, blood, and/or bile.

Assuming you're not someone who gets excited by the word "tripe," think of this slow-simmered tomatoey stew as the gateway to tripeworld. It's a special kind of deliciousness. As the tripe simmers, it thickens the stew like a gravy. Between the luscious texture and rich flavor from the smoked pork hock, you'll end up with a dish that has soul-warming powers. My dad's generation liked to braise meat until it was soft enough to eat with no teeth. I prefer tripe that's tender, but with a pleasant chew to it—something to remind you of what you're eating.

Pastele Stew

- 3 tablespoons neutral oil, plus more as needed
- 3 pounds boneless pork butt or shoulder, cut into ¾-inch cubes
- 2 teaspoons kosher salt, plus more to taste
- 1 large red bell pepper, roughly chopped
- 2 jalapeños, halved and seeded
- 6 cloves garlic, peeled but whole
- 2 medium sweet onions, roughly chopped
- 2 bunches of cilantro
- 1 tablespoon ground cumin
- 1 tablespoon dried oregano
- 1 teaspoon gochugaru (Korean chile flakes) or red chile flakes
- ½ teaspoon freshly ground black pepper, plus more to taste
- ½ teaspoon ground annatto
- 1 large green bell pepper, roughly chopped

In a large pot or Dutch oven, heat 2 tablespoons of the oil over medium-high heat until shimmering. Add the pork and season with the salt. Cook, stirring occasionally, until the pork has browned all over and rendered out some of its fat, 15 to 20 minutes. Make sure to scrape the bottom of the pot as you stir.

Meanwhile, in a food processor or blender, combine the red bell pepper, jalapeños, garlic, half of the chopped onion, 1 bunch of the cilantro (with stems), and the remaining 1 tablespoon oil. Pulse until everything is finely chopped and a loose paste forms. This is your sofrito.

Transfer the browned pork to a plate. There should be a good layer of fat and oil at the bottom of the pot; if not, drizzle in enough oil to completely coat the pot. With the heat still at medium-high, add the cumin, oregano, gochugaru, black pepper, annatto, and the sofrito from the blender. Cook, stirring frequently, until most of the moisture has evaporated and the paste starts to brown on the edges, 3 to 4 minutes.

Add the green bell pepper and the remaining chopped onion and cook, stirring often, until slightly softened, another 3 to 4 minutes.

Return the browned pork to the pot, add the diced tomatoes and tomato sauce, and bring to a boil. Reduce the heat to a simmer,

recipe and ingredients continue →

If you grew up in Hawai'i, you probably have a soft spot for pastele stew. It's a dish that only exists here in the islands—and like many dishes here, there's a miniature history lesson behind it. For those unfamiliar with pasteles, they're to Puerto Rican cuisine what tamales are to Mexican cuisine, made using masa from plantains instead of corn and stuffed with pork. When immigrants from Puerto Rico arrived to work in Hawai'i in the 1900s, they soon found there were no plantains around, so they improvised with green bananas (and sometimes taro) and wrapped them in the ti leaves that were abundant.

The Puerto Rican families we knew could be relied upon for a steady supply of pasteles during the holidays, and we'd occasionally see them sold out of roadside coolers as well. But, as anyone who's made tamales from scratch will tell you, making pasteles is a lot of work, which is where pastele stew comes from. It can be made rather quickly and provides a way to enjoy the flavors of pastele with far less work. These days, the simple everyday stew tends to dominate, and frankly, we're all happy with it.

For pastele stew, the traditional ratio gets flipped—rather than unripe plantains filled with pork, the main element is chunks of pork thickened with grated green bananas. The common bananas found at any supermarket will work in this case, just be sure to grab the most completely green and unripe ones you can find, so they're at their starchiest.

- 1 (14.5-ounce) can diced tomatoes
- 1 (15-ounce) can tomato sauce
- 1 pound very green bananas
- Boiling water, as needed
- 2 (6-ounce) cans black olives, drained
- Tabasco
- Cooked white rice, for serving

SERVES 8

partially cover, and continue cooking, stirring occasionally, for about 10 minutes while you prepare the green bananas.

Trim the ends from the green bananas and slice the skins all the way down lengthwise on each side. Soak the unpeeled green bananas in just-boiled water for 5 minutes, then transfer to a plate (this makes the skin easier to peel). Once cooled, peel the bananas and finely grate (using a box grater) into a large bowl.

After the stew has been simmering for about 10 minutes, stir in the grated bananas, making sure no large clumps remain. Continue cooking, stirring occasionally, until the pork is tender and the stew has thickened, another 20 minutes.

Finely chop the remaining bunch of cilantro and add to the stew, along with the black olives. Cook for another minute or so, just until the olives are heated through. Season with salt, pepper, and Tabasco to taste. Serve hot with rice.

Chef Chris and Auntie Becky Speere at their Huelo home

LOCAL
RUBBER SLIPPERS $12 09
10.5
LOCAL
RUBBER SLIPPERS $12 09
11.5

CHICKEN & SEAFOOD

Shoyu Chicken

1 cup shoyu (soy sauce)

1 cup packed light brown sugar

2-inch piece fresh ginger, sliced and crushed with the butt of a knife

4 cloves garlic, smashed and peeled

2 scallions, roughly chopped, plus more for garnish

1 teaspoon toasted sesame oil

4 pounds bone-in, skin-on chicken thighs

½ teaspoon freshly ground black pepper

1 cup low-sodium chicken broth or water

2 tablespoons cornstarch

Scallion Rice (page 123) or cooked white rice, for serving

SERVES 6

In a 10-inch saucepan, combine the shoyu, brown sugar, ginger, garlic, scallions, and sesame oil. Stir over medium heat until the sugar is dissolved. Just as the mixture starts to boil, remove from the heat.

Once the mixture has cooled, place the chicken thighs into a large resealable plastic bag and pour the marinade over the chicken. Seal and marinate in the fridge for 2 hours, or overnight for the best flavor.

In a large pot or Dutch oven, combine the chicken (with marinade), pepper, and chicken broth and stir to combine. Bring to a boil over medium-high heat. Reduce the heat to low, cover, and cook at a bare simmer until the chicken is tender and cooked through, 35 to 45 minutes, flipping the thighs in the sauce every 10 minutes or so. (If you're using a slow cooker, cook on the low setting for 4 to 5 hours, until it's thoroughly cooked but not falling apart into strands.)

Remove the chicken from the pot and set aside. If you like, you can remove and discard the chunks of ginger, garlic, and scallion with a slotted spoon or spider strainer. Raise the heat and bring the sauce to a boil. In a small bowl, whisk the cornstarch with 2 tablespoons cold water to form a slurry, then slowly stir into the boiling sauce. Continue stirring until the sauce has thickened, 1 to 2 minutes.

Remove from the heat, return the chicken to the pot, and serve warm with scallion rice.

Shoyu chicken is the king of the Hawai'i potluck. As they say in fantasy football, it's got a high floor as a dish—and I'd say a high ceiling, too. No one will ever complain if you bring even mediocre shoyu chicken to a party, but if you show up with this succulent version that makes everyone mop their plate and go back for thirds, you're guaranteed high praise.

An easy way to think of shoyu chicken is as a slowly simmered, almost poached, version of teriyaki—there are some differences, of course, but the combination of flavors is similar. And since I believe it's easier to simmer something than grill it, this is the can't-mess-up chicken recipe I would give first to any burgeoning home cook. You can even use a slow cooker to set it and forget it. And if you end up with leftover sauce, use it for a shortcut version of Shoyu Hot Dogs (page 41).

Rotisserie Chicken Kelaguen

1½ pounds cooked chicken, skin removed and finely chopped (from 1 whole rotisserie chicken)

1 small red onion, finely chopped

½ cup fresh lemon juice, plus more to taste

¼ cup thinly sliced scallions

3 cloves garlic, minced

2 to 3 small hot chiles (optional), such as Thai or Hawaiian chiles, finely chopped

1 teaspoon kosher salt, plus more to taste

½ teaspoon freshly ground black pepper

1 cup frozen grated coconut (see Note), thawed

Flour tortillas, white rice, or butter crackers (optional), for serving

Tabasco or hot sauce of choice (optional), for serving

SERVES 4

In a large nonreactive bowl, combine the chopped chicken, red onion, lemon juice, scallions, garlic, chiles (if using), salt, and black pepper. Stir to combine. Add the grated coconut and fold to combine. Taste and season with more salt and lemon juice as needed. Cover and refrigerate for at least 1 hour and up to overnight before serving.

Serve chilled or at room temperature with flour tortillas, warm rice, or crackers, plus hot sauce if you like.

Kelaguen (nearly rhymes with *pelican*) is a dish that comes from the Chamorro, the Indigenous people of Guam and the Mariana Islands. Hawai'i is home to over six thousand Chamorros, and if you invite one of them to a potluck, there's a good chance that they'll bring some kelaguen to the party. A cousin of ceviche, it's made by marinating meat of some kind (most commonly chicken) in citrus juice, then tossing it with onions, spicy chiles, and creamy grated coconut.

Traditionally, kelaguen is made with grilled chicken. Most people I know who make it in Hawai'i, however, use grocery-store rotisserie chicken instead, a time-saving, leftover-friendly hack that makes it an instant weeknight staple. Though the flavor is bright and acidic, the grated coconut adds a fresh richness that makes me think of chicken salad. It's fantastic eaten on its own, but for a complete meal, serve it with thick flour tortillas (a substitute for a Chamorro flatbread called titiyas), some warm rice, or with butter crackers for scooping.

Note: Frozen grated coconut can be found in most Asian or Latin grocery stores, but you can also substitute the same quantity of unsweetened shredded (desiccated) coconut that's been soaked in a 13-ounce can of unsweetened coconut milk for 15 minutes, then drained.

"Take Along" Hibachi Chicken or Shrimp

- 1 cup mayonnaise
- 2 tablespoons sugar
- 2 tablespoons oyster sauce
- 2 tablespoons minced garlic
- 1 tablespoon finely chopped fresh parsley
- Grated zest and juice of 1 lemon
- ½ teaspoon freshly ground black pepper
- 3 pounds boneless, skinless chicken thighs, or easy-peel jumbo shrimp (thawed if frozen)
- Skewers (optional)
- Neutral oil, for the grill
- Kosher salt

SERVES 4 TO 6

In a large bowl or resealable bag, combine the mayo, sugar, oyster sauce, garlic, parsley, lemon zest, lemon juice, and pepper. Mix thoroughly. If you're using shrimp, it's worth placing the shrimp on skewers (spaced out slightly so the marinade can reach each one) before marinating them. Add the chicken or shrimp and toss, making sure they're completely coated. Marinate, in the fridge or a cooler, for at least 1 hour, or up to 2 to 3 days.

When ready to cook, prepare a grill for high direct heat or preheat a grill pan on the stovetop. Using tongs and an oiled rag or paper towels, oil the grates of the grill or the grill pan.

Place the chicken or shrimp directly on the grill, without shaking off any excess marinade (it should cling to the meat). Season the top side with a pinch of salt, then season the second side with another pinch after you flip it.

For chicken

Grill the thighs, uncovered, until they are charred and browned on both sides, easily released from the grates, and are cooked through (until the center reads at least 165°F on a probe thermometer), 4 to 6 minutes per side.

For shrimp

Grill the shrimp until browned and slightly charred on both sides and cooked through, 2 to 3 minutes on each side.

Serve hot from the grill. Utensils and plates optional.

The first time I came upon this recipe, I was thumbing through an old local cookbook. I'd never heard of it, but the idea seemed smart: a no-fuss, forgiving marinade that imparts lots of flavor but won't turn your meat rubbery or mushy if it sits long, as can happen with marinades with a lot of salt or acid. The secret here is the addition of mayo, which both protects the meat from curing too much and helps form a nice crust once grilled.

The name "take along" comes from the notion that you can toss it in your ice cooler when you're camping or fishing and forget about it for a few hours—or days—until you're ready to grill. The funny thing is, once I started mentioning this recipe to guys around my dad's age, they all knew what I was talking about. They just didn't have a name for it.

My take on this garlicky-lemony marinade is hard to mess up, provided you take care on a few minor details that will help produce flavorful, juicy chicken or shrimp. First, make sure your grill is good and hot. These proteins are better grilled hard and fast, so the mayo and sugar form a charred, caramelized crust rather than melt off, and the interior remains plump. If you let the marinade sit longer than 12 hours, it can cause the meat to cook quicker than usual, so be careful to not overcook. Also, since the marinade doesn't contain an excess of salt, I like to bring some along to sprinkle over the finished product, but that's up to you.

Miso-Peanut Hibachi Chicken

¼ cup shiro (white) miso

¼ cup creamy peanut butter

¼ cup shoyu (soy sauce)

¼ cup packed light brown sugar

¼ cup beer, any kind (a standard lager is my go-to)

3 cloves garlic, minced or grated

2 teaspoons sriracha or chili garlic paste (optional)

2½ pounds boneless, skinless chicken thighs

Oil, for the grill

SERVES 4 TO 6

In a large bowl or resealable bag, mix together the miso, peanut butter, shoyu, brown sugar, beer, garlic, and sriracha (if using) until combined. Add the chicken and toss to coat. Marinate in the fridge overnight.

When ready to cook, prepare a grill for high direct heat or preheat a grill pan on the stovetop. Using tongs and an oiled rag or paper towels, oil the grates of the grill or grill pan.

Place the chicken directly on the grill, without shaking off any excess marinade. Grill the thighs, uncovered, until they are charred and browned on both sides, easily released from the grates, and are cooked through (until the center reads at least 165°F on a probe thermometer), 4 to 6 minutes per side. Serve immediately.

Sam Choy is one of the most admired chefs from Hawai'i ever, and a huge influence on me since what we'd call *small kid time*. I always wanted to cook like Sam. A born and raised O'ahu boy, the big Sam is famous for many things—his down-home cooking style, his mastery of poke, and his love of aloha shirts—but maybe more than anything, his miso-peanut butter chicken. Though I doubt he'd claim to have invented it (he's humble like that), the recipe first appeared in one of his cookbooks many decades ago and became incredibly popular seemingly overnight. Suddenly it was in newspapers and on TV and everyone knew how to make it.

It's maintained its staying power ever since and I think it's because there's something about the combination of miso and peanut butter and how it caramelizes when it hits the grill that's just incredible. You can smell it a full mile away when someone is grilling it at the beach. My twist is adding a little spicy chili paste to the mix, which doesn't add heat as much as it does add a little sharpness that balances the rich flavors. Since the marinade clings to the meat almost like a crust, leaner chicken breasts can work here, too, but to me there's nothing that beats the juiciness and even-cooking of boneless, skinless thighs on the hibachi.

Chicken Inasal

For the marinated chicken

2 cups apple cider vinegar

Juice of 1 orange

½ cup shoyu (soy sauce)

½ cup packed light brown sugar

12 cloves garlic, smashed and peeled

1 tablespoon kosher salt

1 teaspoon freshly ground black pepper

4-inch piece fresh ginger, roughly chopped and smashed

2 stalks lemongrass, trimmed and smashed

6 skin-on chicken leg quarters

Marinate the chicken: In a medium bowl, combine the vinegar, orange juice, shoyu, brown sugar, garlic, salt, and pepper and whisk until the sugar is dissolved. Place the ginger, lemongrass, and chicken quarters in a large resealable bag and cover with the marinade, then seal and squeeze out the air. Marinate in the fridge for at least 4 hours and up to 12 hours (any longer and the vinegar will affect the chicken's texture), massaging the bag once or twice to mix everything.

One hour before you're ready to cook, remove the chicken from the fridge and let it come to room temperature.

recipe and ingredients continue →

Filipinos—especially Filipinos in Hawai'i—love grilling anything they can get their hands on. The sight of meat or fish charring over hot coals and that intoxicating smell that clings to your hair or clothes stir something in us. There's rarely an occasion, big or small, where cooking "Filipino BBQ" isn't just a welcome activity, but an expected one. So when I describe chicken inasal as "grilled chicken," that might be underselling it a bit. This isn't just any old grilled chicken.

My favorite style of inasal is a famous Ilonggo dish from the islands of the Visayas. It's marinated with layers of citrus, vinegar, lemongrass, garlic, and ginger that infuses a sweet and tangy brine into the meat, then it's slowly grilled over charcoal and basted with achuete (also known as achiote or annatto) oil, which adds a subtle earthiness and a ruddy red color to the charred skin, then served with chile-spiked toyomansi.

When firing up your grill (use charcoal for the best flavor), keep in mind that the cooking surface will have hotter and cooler spots. I like to start over the hottest portion to develop some pleasant bits of char on the skin, then transfer it to the cooler side and cover the grill so the meat cooks more quickly and evenly via oven-like indirect heat. That said, I always maintain there's no such thing as turning and rotating your meat too much on the grill, so the important part is to watch your chicken, move it around the hot spots as needed, and just make sure it doesn't burn.

Chicken thighs are an acceptable substitute here, but if you're going to the trouble of making the marinade, I would strongly recommend using chicken leg quarters (with the thigh and leg attached). The vinegar and citrus work to soften and break down all the connective bits and cartilage, and you'll end up with a very succulent and juicy piece of grilled chicken. Feel free to serve a big bowl of rice on the side if you want—for me, though, the best partner for inasal is a cold beer.

Note: The key ingredient in an excellent chicken inasal marinade is acidity (in this case, milder-tasting apple cider vinegar and citrus), which helps tenderize the meat while adding a tangy flavor complement from the floral aroma of lemongrass and the punch of black pepper, ginger, and garlic. There is a sweet spot to the marinade time—I aim for at least 4 hours to ensure absorption, but after 12 hours the vinegar can start to break down the fibers in the chicken and turn the meat mushy. Basting the chicken often with the annatto oil is crucial, too, as it ensures the meat stays moist and develops a gorgeous glistening skin. More basting is better in this case.

For the basting oil

½ cup neutral oil

1 teaspoon ground annatto or smoked paprika

2 tablespoons salted butter

2 tablespoons shoyu (soy sauce)

2 tablespoons fresh lime juice

Grated zest of 1 orange

For the dipping sauce

Toyomansi (page 256)

Small hot chiles, such as Thai or Hawaiian chiles, stemmed and lightly crushed (optional)

SERVES 6

Meanwhile, prepare the basting oil: In a small pot, combine the oil and annatto and stir over medium heat until the powder has dissolved and the oil has turned a deep red color, about a minute. Add the butter and stir until melted, then remove the pot from the heat and let cool. Once cooled to room temperature, stir in the shoyu, lime juice, and orange zest.

Make the dipping sauce: In a small bowl, mix the toyomansi with a few whole chiles to taste (if using). Set aside until ready to serve.

Prepare a grill for high indirect heat (for a charcoal grill, push the coals to one side; for a gas grill, leave one or two burners off). Using tongs and an oil rag or paper towels, oil the grates of the grill.

When the grill is hot, set the chicken skin-side down on the direct heat side of the grill. Once the chicken has some char and grill marks and releases easily from the grates, 2 to 3 minutes, move the chicken over indirect heat, still skin-side down. Cover the grill and cook, turning the chicken every couple of minutes and basting frequently with the annatto oil, until the juices run clear or an instant-read thermometer inserted into the thickest part of the thigh registers 160°F, another 8 to 10 minutes. The chicken should spend about three-quarters of its grilling time skin-side down, which will create a nice, browned crust. If the skin is browning too quickly, move it farther away from the heat source.

Transfer to a serving platter (or cutting board) and let rest for 10 minutes. Serve warm with the dipping sauce.

Crispy Chicken Thighs
with Sinigang Dust

For the crispy chicken

¼ cup cornstarch

2 tablespoons shoyu (soy sauce)

2 tablespoons granulated sugar

1-inch piece fresh ginger, grated

1 tablespoon fish sauce

1 teaspoon garlic powder

1 teaspoon toasted sesame oil

½ teaspoon freshly ground black pepper

½ teaspoon ground white pepper

2 pounds boneless, skinless chicken thighs

For the sinigang dust

1 tablespoon tomato-chicken bouillon powder or chicken bouillon powder

2 teaspoons citric acid or lemon powder

1 teaspoon light brown sugar

1 teaspoon onion powder

½ teaspoon ground turmeric

To finish

Neutral oil, for frying

Cooked white rice, for serving

SERVES 4 TO 6

Prepare the crispy chicken: In a small bowl, combine the cornstarch, shoyu, granulated sugar, ginger, fish sauce, garlic powder, sesame oil, black pepper, and white pepper. Mix well. Place the thighs in a shallow dish or large resealable bag and pour the marinade over the chicken. Make sure the chicken is coated well. Marinate in the fridge for at least 2 hours (or overnight for best flavor).

Meanwhile, make the sinigang dust: In a small bowl, stir together the bouillon powder, citric acid, brown sugar, onion powder, and turmeric until combined. Taste and adjust as needed: you should get a zing of sourness up front, but it should be balanced by saltiness, savoriness, and sweetness as well. Set aside.

Remove the marinated chicken from the fridge about 30 minutes before you start cooking.

Pour ¼ inch of oil into a 12-inch skillet and heat over medium-high heat until shimmering. Working in batches, add the chicken thighs in a single layer and cook, turning once, until the internal temperature reaches 165°F on an instant-read thermometer, about 6 minutes per side. Transfer the fried thighs to a plate and, while still warm, sprinkle both sides liberally with the sinigang dust.

Serve immediately over rice.

Sinigang is a traditional Filipino sour soup that's made with tamarind or other acidic ingredients like tart citrus or vinegar. If you've had it before, you know that *zing* moment when the broth hits your tongue and immediately draws you back for another spoonful. Here that trademark twang is captured in the spice blend used to coat these crispy, marinated, shallow-fried chicken thighs. If you live near an Asian grocery, the most straightforward method would be to use the packaged sinigang soup mix (which you'd find in the cupboard of any of my aunties and uncles). But since those mixes are mainly a mixture of salt, MSG, and citric acid, which provides the sourness, with only a nominal amount of tamarind powder, you're just as well off making your own sour seasoning from scratch. If you don't already have citric acid on hand, it's an inexpensive and versatile pantry addition that lasts forever and adds the same acidic flavor found in all citrus juice, without the liquid.

Sweet & Sour Tsukune

For the meatballs

1 pound ground chicken

¼ cup minced white onion

1 large egg, lightly beaten

1 tablespoon cornstarch

1 tablespoon toasted sesame oil

1 tablespoon shiro (white) miso

½ teaspoon grated fresh ginger

½ teaspoon kosher salt

¼ teaspoon ground white pepper

Neutral oil, as needed

For the stir-fry

1 (20-ounce) can juice-packed pineapple chunks

Neutral oil, for frying

½ medium white onion, cut into wedges and separated

1 large green bell pepper, chopped

1 medium carrot, peeled and thinly sliced into coins

2 teaspoons chicken bouillon powder

For the sweet and sour sauce

⅓ cup ketchup

¼ cup shoyu (soy sauce)

2 tablespoons rice vinegar

2 tablespoons brown sugar

1 tablespoon cornstarch

Cooked white rice, for serving

SERVES 4

Make the meatballs: In a large bowl, combine the ground chicken, onion, egg, cornstarch, sesame oil, miso, ginger, salt, and white pepper. Knead the mixture with your hands until it's mixed well and very sticky. Apply a small amount of oil to your hands and roll out balls the size of Ping-Pong balls with the mixture (or use a cookie dough scooper).

In a wide saucepan or skillet with a lid, add a generous tablespoon of neutral oil and enough water to cover the bottom of the pan by ½ inch. Set over medium heat and once the water is boiling, carefully add the meatballs to the pan. Cover and cook for 5 minutes, turning the meatballs halfway through. Uncover, increase the heat to medium-high, and continue to cook the meatballs, turning regularly, until the water evaporates and the meatballs are browned on all sides, another 5 to 6 minutes. Transfer the browned meatballs to a plate. Hold on to the pan for the stir-fry.

Cook the stir-fry: Reserving the juice for the sweet and sour sauce, drain the pineapple chunks. Add 1 tablespoon of oil to the pan and heat until shimmering. Add the pineapple chunks, onion wedges, bell pepper, carrot, and bouillon powder. Stir-fry until the vegetables just start to soften, 2 to 3 minutes. Transfer the vegetables to the plate with the meatballs.

Make the sweet and sour sauce: Add the reserved pineapple juice to the pan, bring to a boil, then lower to a simmer for a few minutes to reduce.

While the pineapple juice is simmering, in a small bowl, whisk together the ketchup, shoyu, vinegar, brown sugar, and cornstarch until smooth.

Pour the mixture into the pineapple juice and simmer, stirring often, until the sauce is thickened and clings to the spoon, about 5 minutes.

Return the meatballs and vegetables to the pan, stirring to coat. Once everything is combined and heated thoroughly, remove the pan from the heat and serve hot with white rice.

A weeknight classic in the Simeon household, sweet and sour meatballs offer a lot of versatility. They're fast to cook, fancy enough to bring to a potluck, and an affordable one-pan meal that pleases both kids and adults. Usually, against my better judgment, we make them with those frozen meatballs that come in bags (which I won't pretend aren't tasty), but I've found that Japanese-style chicken meatballs are a lighter, lower-in-fat option that don't sacrifice juiciness or flavor. Start by searing the meatballs, then stir-fry your daily quota of veggies, and build the sweet and sour sauce in the pan before returning the meatballs for a brief final simmer.

Chinese Kanpachi Crudo

2-inch piece fresh ginger, peeled

2 scallions, trimmed

½ pound skinless sushi-grade kanpachi fillet

2 tablespoons shoyu (soy sauce)

1 tablespoon fresh lemon juice

2 teaspoons chili crisp or Nori Salsa Macha (page 255)

2 tablespoons peanut oil or other neutral oil

2 teaspoons toasted sesame oil

Flaky salt, such as Maldon

Cilantro leaves or microgreens, for garnish

SERVES 4

Before you start, place a large plate or serving platter in the fridge to chill.

Fill a small bowl with ice and water. Julienne the ginger into thin matchstick-like pieces and place in the ice water. Cut the scallions crosswise into 2-inch sections, then julienne into thin matchstick-like pieces and place in the ice water. Let soak for 5 minutes while you prepare the fish.

Using a very sharp knife and cutting in a sweeping motion (rather than sawing), cut the fish into ¼-inch slices. Arrange the slices on the chilled plate, overlapping them very slightly, then return the plate to the fridge while you prepare the dressing.

In a small bowl, whisk together the shoyu, lemon juice, and chili crisp. Set the dressing aside.

Drain and pat dry the ginger and scallion. Remove the sashimi plate from the fridge. Top the sashimi with the ginger and scallion matchsticks so you get a few pieces of each with each slice of fish (you may not use all of it).

In a small saucepan, heat the peanut oil with the sesame oil over medium-high heat until it begins to smoke, about 2 minutes. Carefully drizzle the hot oil over the sashimi pieces, then use a spoon to drizzle the shoyu-chili dressing over the top. Sprinkle each slice of sashimi with flaky salt, then garnish with cilantro leaves. Serve immediately.

Making crudo or sashimi at home can somehow be both intimidating and boring. You paid a lot of money for a nice slab of raw fish and don't want to mess it up, so you season it as gingerly as possible, and surprise, it's nowhere as exciting as what's at the sushi place in town.

I'd like to think this gorgeous sashimi—which is essentially a raw fish version of traditional Chinese steamed whole fish—solves that issue with light effort. Right before serving, the fish is drizzled with hot oil, which activates the aromas of ginger and scallions arranged over the top, sending a delicious smell into the air, and adds a bit of tableside flair. The key is to serve the sashimi on a dish that's been chilled in the fridge. Once the oil warms the plate slightly, the fish will be the ideal temperature to bring out its flavor. If you're unable to find kanpachi, try substituting sushi-grade yellowtail, mahimahi, halibut, or even salmon.

Panko Fish Sandwiches

For the tartar sauce

¾ cup mayonnaise

½ cup sweet relish

2 tablespoons finely minced sweet onion

1 tablespoon finely chopped fresh dill or 2 teaspoons dried dill

1 tablespoon capers, drained and finely chopped

1 teaspoon Dijon mustard

1 teaspoon garlic powder

½ teaspoon kosher salt, plus more to taste

½ teaspoon freshly ground black pepper, plus more to taste

For the panko fish

4 mahimahi fillets (4 to 5 ounces each) or other firm whitefish, such as cod or flounder

Garlic salt

Freshly ground black pepper

1 cup all-purpose flour

¼ cup mayonnaise

1 tablespoon Dijon mustard

2 cups panko bread crumbs

Neutral oil, for frying

For serving

4 soft brioche buns, split

Shredded iceberg lettuce (optional)

4 slices American cheese

MAKES 4 SANDWICHES

Make the tartar sauce: In a small bowl, combine the mayo, sweet relish, onion, dill, capers, mustard, garlic powder, salt, and pepper. Stir well to combine. Adjust with more salt and pepper to taste, then cover and refrigerate for at least 30 minutes and up to overnight to allow the flavors to meld.

Make the panko fish: Season the fish with garlic salt and pepper on both sides.

Set up a breading station with three shallow bowls: Fill one with the all-purpose flour. In a second, whisk together the mayo, mustard, and ¼ cup cold water. Spread the panko in the third.

Dredge each mahimahi fillet in the flour, shake off the excess, then coat it in the mayo mixture, letting any extra drip back into the dish. Finally, coat it evenly with panko bread crumbs. Transfer the fillets to a plate as you finish them.

Line a plate with paper towels and have it near the stove. Pour ¼ inch oil into a 12-inch skillet and heat over medium-high heat until shimmering.

Fry the fillets until golden brown on both sides and cooked through, 2 to 3 minutes per side—the exact time will depend on the thickness of the fillets. Transfer the fish to the paper towels.

Serve the sandwiches: Wipe any remaining oil and bread crumbs from the skillet and place over medium-low heat. Toast the brioche buns lightly on both the cut sides and the outsides.

For each sandwich, spread a dollop of tartar sauce on a bottom bun and top with a handful of iceberg lettuce (if using). Place a fish fillet on top and cover with a slice of cheese. Dollop on a little more tartar sauce and cover with the top bun. Serve immediately.

At Tin Roof, we're constantly running weekly specials, and this one has always been a huge hit whenever we put it on the menu board. The toppings are simple, so what makes this fried fish sandwich special is the pop of flavor that comes from making your own tartar sauce. Everyone knows what tartar sauce from a squeeze bottle tastes like, but when you make it fresh with bright herbs, salty capers, and crunchy, snappy pickled things, you begin to understand on a deeper level why this tangy, creamy, textured sauce is famous for being fried fish's best friend. That said, if you want to squeeze away, I'm not here to judge you.

Tomato–Black Pepper Sardine Banh Mi

Pickled Daikon and Carrots (recipe follows)

½ large seedless cucumber, thinly sliced

Handful of cilantro sprigs

¼ cup mayonnaise

1 teaspoon Maggi sauce (or shoyu/soy sauce with a pinch of chicken bouillon)

1 baguette, halved crosswise and split open, or two 8- to 10-inch crusty rolls, split open (see Note)

2 tablespoons extra-virgin olive oil

2 cloves garlic, thinly sliced

2 (4-ounce) cans sardines in tomato sauce

Sriracha sauce

Freshly ground black pepper

MAKES 2 SANDWICHES

Make the daikon and carrot pickles at least 1 hour ahead (or make well ahead, as they will keep in the fridge for a couple of weeks).

Arrange the cucumber, cilantro, and daikon and carrot pickles on a work surface so they're easily accessible. In a small bowl, stir together the mayo and Maggi sauce until combined and set aside.

In a medium skillet, warm the baguettes over medium-high heat until heated through and soft on both sides. Remove the baguettes from the pan and set aside.

Add the oil to the skillet and heat until it begins to shimmer. Add the garlic. Pop open the sardine cans and use a fork to carefully add the whole fillets to the pan (as best you can), reserving the sauce. Sear the sardines on each side until lightly browned, flipping them after about 1 minute.

Add a generous squirt of sriracha to the reserved tomato sauce, then pour the sauce into the skillet and baste the seared sardines with it, cooking until the sauce is reduced, 2 to 3 minutes total. Season the sardines with lots of black pepper, then remove the pan from the heat.

Spread an ample amount of mayo-Maggi sauce onto each baguette, then layer with the cucumber slices and daikon and carrot pickles. Divide the sardines between the sandwiches, then add the cilantro. Serve immediately.

recipe continues →

When restaurants were closed at the start of the pandemic, I started doing something that I almost never did during two-plus decades working in restaurant kitchens: making lunch at home. And in the process, I learned to appreciate something that all restaurant cooks take for granted but that gets overlooked by most home cooks, which is setting up a station.

A sandwich shop, let's say a banh mi shop to be specific, is a perfect example. The sandwich maker likely has an assembly line of ingredients before them, which allows them to move from station to station and build multiple sandwiches quickly.

I take the same approach for making one of my go-to lunches at home, the sardine banh mi. Making a half-dozen of these sandwiches takes about as much time as making just two if you set up stations, so it's a great option to feed several hungry people when short on time. And best yet, most of the work is done by popping a tin can.

My favorite sardines to use are the ones packed in tomato sauce (or even better, spicy tomato sauce). That way the flavorful sauce can be doctored up and used as another layer of seasoning, while the drained sardines get seared in the pan until their skins are crispy. The only advanced planning this sandwich requires is the pickled daikon and carrots, which can be done in the late morning and be ready by lunchtime on the short end, or several days in advance if you prefer.

After you've laid out all the toppings, all that's left to do is briefly cook the sardines and run them through the banh mi assembly-line setup before you.

Note: Stale baguette? Run the crusty bread under the faucet briefly so it gets slightly damp, then stick it in a 300°F oven for 5 to 7 minutes. The inside will regain its moisture and the outside will stay crackly crisp.

Pickled Daikon and Carrots MAKES ABOUT 2 CUPS

½ pound daikon radish, peeled and cut into thin matchsticks (about 1 cup)

½ pound carrots, peeled and cut into thin matchsticks (about 1 cup)

1 tablespoon kosher salt

1 cup rice vinegar

¾ cup sugar

In a medium bowl, toss the daikon and carrots with the salt until combined. Let sit for 20 minutes.

Meanwhile, in a small saucepan, combine the vinegar, sugar, and ½ cup water. Stir over high heat just until the sugar is completely dissolved, then remove from the heat and place in the fridge or freezer to cool completely.

Once the 20 minutes is up, rinse the daikon and carrots well with water, drain, and transfer to a lidded jar. Pour the cooled vinegar mixture over the top and place the pickles in the fridge. Chill for at least 1 hour before using. The leftovers will keep in the fridge for 2 to 3 weeks.

My daughter Quinn with a golden tilapia caught out of the Speeres' home pond

Salt & Pepper Fish Sticks

- 2 teaspoons sugar
- 1 teaspoon chicken bouillon powder
- 1 teaspoon gochugaru (Korean chile flakes) or red chile flakes, or to taste
- ½ teaspoon kosher salt
- ½ teaspoon ground white pepper
- Neutral oil
- 1 pound frozen fish sticks, or frozen battered fillets halved lengthwise
- ¼ medium sweet onion, sliced into quarter moons
- 1 tablespoon minced fresh ginger
- 4 cloves garlic, thinly sliced
- ½ medium jalapeño, thinly sliced
- ¼ cup thinly sliced scallions
- ¼ cup torn basil leaves (optional)

SERVES 2 TO 4

In a small bowl, mix together the sugar, bouillon powder, gochugaru, salt, and white pepper. Set the seasoning mixture aside.

Line a plate with paper towels and have it near the stove. Drizzle just enough oil into a large skillet to lightly coat the bottom of the pan. Set over medium-high heat and once the oil starts to shimmer, add the frozen fish sticks and cook until heated through and golden brown, 3 to 5 minutes on each side, depending on the thickness of the fish. Transfer the fish sticks to the paper towels and set aside.

In the same skillet still over medium-high heat, drizzle in enough oil to lightly coat the bottom of the pan once more. Once the oil is very hot (starting to smoke), add the onion, ginger, and garlic and stir-fry for 15 to 20 seconds, until fragrant and lightly browned. Add the jalapeño and stir-fry for another 15 to 20 seconds, until slightly softened.

Return the fish sticks to the pan and sprinkle them with the reserved seasoning mixture, gently tossing and flipping the fish sticks with a spatula so they're evenly coated but stay intact. Remove the pan from the heat and toss in the scallions and basil (if using). Serve immediately.

I love the technique in Chinese cuisine of using a dry wok to cook things hot and fast, which adds that elusive seared, smoky flavor known as wok hei and just generally makes things delicious in a short amount of time. A good example of this are Cantonese "salt-and-pepper" (the "pepper" usually means a mild chile) stir-fries, where you're taking a cooked or fried protein and engulfing it with seasonings in a hot pan with only a very little oil in order to infuse it with flavor and fragrance. The coolest part is that this technique also works with things you might usually crisp up in an oven or air fryer, including frozen fish sticks! The blueprint of spices and aromatics in this recipe can be applied to any cooked protein that lends itself to being crisped up, like seared or fried tofu, leftover steak, seafood, even chicken tenders if you're feeling a little wild.

Lemon Caper Mahi

Neutral oil, for pan-frying

4 medium mahimahi fillets (about 4 ounces each)

Kosher salt and freshly ground black pepper

¼ cup all-purpose flour

2 tablespoons salted butter

1 small shallot, minced (about 2 tablespoons)

2 teaspoons grated fresh ginger

1 heaping tablespoon capers, drained and roughly chopped

½ cup dry white wine or sake

Juice of 1 lemon

¼ cup half-and-half

2 teaspoons finely chopped fresh parsley

SERVES 2 TO 4

Add just enough oil to a large skillet to coat the bottom of the pan and set it over medium-high heat.

While the pan is heating, pat the fillets dry and season generously on each side with salt and pepper. Spread the flour onto a plate or tray, then dredge the fillets in the flour, coating them all over and shaking off any excess flour.

Once the oil in the pan is shimmering, add the fillets to the pan, making sure there's enough space so that they don't touch. After about 10 seconds, use a spatula to firmly press the fish into the pan, then carefully scrape them up to loosen them from the pan. Don't worry if they stick slightly—this step helps form a better crust.

Continue cooking the fish undisturbed for 3 to 4 minutes (depending on the thickness of the fillets) until a golden-brown crust forms. Then carefully flip the fish, add 1 tablespoon of the butter to the pan, and cook for another 90 seconds to 2 minutes, using a spoon to baste the fish with butter as it finishes cooking. The fish should end up cooked medium-well: It will flake easily with a fork but is still soft and tender.

Remove the pan from the heat and transfer the fish to a serving plate, drizzling the browned butter over the top.

Return the pan to the stove and reduce the heat to medium. Add the shallot, ginger, and capers and stir-fry for about 1 minute, until the shallots have softened slightly and the ginger and capers are fragrant, making sure to scrape up any browned bits in the pan. Add the white wine and lemon juice. Once the liquid has reduced by about half, 1 to 2 minutes, add the half-and-half and season with a pinch of salt and pepper.

Remove the pan from the heat and add the remaining 1 tablespoon butter and half of the parsley, stirring until the butter is melted and the sauce is glossy and slightly thickened. To serve, spoon the pan sauce over the fillets and sprinkle with the remaining parsley.

My brother, Jeremy, who also works in the food service industry, is to mahimahi what Bubba from *Forrest Gump* was to shrimp. Fried, grilled, broiled, loco moco'd—if he sees it on the menu, game over. That's what he's ordering.

He's not the only person with a strong affection for this Hawaiian favorite that's a prized catch among sport fishers (its name translates to "very strong"). It has a mild but rich taste, and it holds up well when cooking (you can take it as far as medium-well and it will remain moist and flaky). Of all the ways to prepare mahimahi—and Jeremy would agree here—lemon caper mahi is king. I love it because not only is the combination of tart lemon and salty capers a clear winner but it's also a textbook example of how a basic pan sauce is a cheat code for cooking restaurant-quality dishes at home.

Sizzling Salmon Sisig

2 tablespoons neutral oil, plus more as needed

10 ounces cooked salmon, flaked, or two (5-ounce) cans salmon, drained and flaked

3 cloves garlic, minced

1 tablespoon minced fresh ginger

1 small jalapeño or serrano, seeded and finely chopped

2 to 3 small hot chiles (optional), such as Thai or Hawaiian chiles, finely chopped

4 teaspoons sugar

1 tablespoon shoyu (soy sauce), plus more to taste

1 small red onion, finely chopped

¼ cup mayonnaise

2 teaspoons fresh lemon juice

Freshly ground black pepper

2 scallions, thinly sliced

2 tablespoons finely crushed pork rinds or fried onions (optional)

Cooked white rice, for serving

Lemon wedges, for squeezing

SERVES 2 TO 4

Line a plate with paper towels and have it near the stove. In a large skillet, heat the oil over medium-high heat until shimmering. Add the salmon flakes and stir-fry until the fish is crispy and browned, 3 to 4 minutes. Transfer to the paper towels and set aside.

In the same skillet, drizzle in just enough oil to coat the pan. Once the oil is shimmering, add the garlic, ginger, jalapeño, and hot chiles (if using). Stir-fry until the ginger and garlic are fragrant and the chiles start to soften, about 30 seconds. Return the salmon to the pan, along with the sugar and shoyu, tossing to combine. Continue cooking until any remaining liquid has evaporated, about another minute.

Transfer the crispy salmon mixture to a bowl and add the red onion, mayo, lemon juice, and a big pinch of black pepper, tossing well to combine. Once everything is incorporated, add the scallions and pork rinds (if using) and give a final toss. Serve immediately with rice and lemon wedges for squeezing over the top.

Sisig is a salty-sour Filipino hash that's usually made from porky bits cooked in a ripping-hot pan until it browns and crackles. Aside from being proof of our love for all things pork, it's a dish that's fundamentally meant to turn leftovers into something special. And cold salmon from the night before is exactly the kind of leftover sisig was destined to help. Since the salmon is already cooked, your goal is to get it sizzling and crispy in a hot pan, then toss it with punchy seasonings to amplify the flavor—garlic, ginger, chiles, red onion, a dollop of mayo for richness. If you don't have leftover fish, use this to make canned salmon a million times more exciting.

Salmon Karaage

¼ cup shoyu (soy sauce)

¼ cup sake

1 tablespoon sugar

2-inch piece fresh ginger, grated

2 pounds salmon fillet, skin removed, cut into two-bite-size chunks

Neutral oil, for frying

¾ cup cornstarch

Shichimi togarashi (optional)

Toyomansi (page 256), for serving

Lemon wedges, for squeezing

SERVES 4 TO 6

In a large bowl, combine the shoyu, sake, sugar, and ginger. Add the salmon pieces to the marinade, tossing so they are well coated. Let it marinate for about 30 minutes in the fridge.

Line a plate with paper towels and have it near the stove. In a large pot or Dutch oven deep enough for frying, heat about ½ inch of oil over medium-high heat until a thermometer reads 350°F. (Or dip the handle of a wooden spoon or a chopstick into the oil. If the oil starts steadily bubbling, then the oil is hot enough for frying.)

Remove the marinated salmon from the fridge. Put the cornstarch in a medium bowl or dish and coat each piece in cornstarch, shaking off any excess. Working in batches to avoid overcrowding, carefully lower the coated salmon into the oil and fry until the salmon is golden and cooked through, flipping often, 3 to 4 minutes. Transfer to the paper towels to drain.

If using, sprinkle the freshly fried salmon with shichimi togarashi for an extra kick. Serve with toyomansi for dipping and lemon wedges for squeezing over the top.

Karaoke. Karate. Katana. Lots of cool Japanese words start with "K," including my favorite, karaage. This streamlined Japanese method of frying is a mainstay of both my kids at home and our work "kids" who run the front counter at Tin Roof, who over the years have come up with every variation of karaage you could possibly imagine and served it as a special.

Karaage is often made with chicken marinated in soy and sake, then tossed in some kind of starch before being fried, but it's also fantastic made with salmon, which tends to hold up well when frying. You can absolutely deep-fry these, but I've had success with a shallow-fry on both sides, which yield crispy fish but means less oil to clean up. Since salmon cooks quickly, make sure the oil is kept over fairly high heat, so you end up with a golden-brown crust but fish that's flaky and moist inside.

Shrimp Egg Foo Young

For the gravy

1 tablespoon neutral oil

4 scallions, finely chopped, white parts only (reserve the greens for the omelets)

1 cup low-sodium chicken broth

2 tablespoons oyster sauce

1 tablespoon shoyu (soy sauce)

2 teaspoons sugar

1 teaspoon apple cider vinegar

1 tablespoon cornstarch

½ teaspoon toasted sesame oil

Kosher salt

Ground white pepper or freshly ground black pepper

Make the gravy: In a small saucepan, heat the neutral oil over medium heat until shimmering. Add the scallion whites and cook, stirring often, until fragrant and softened, about 1 minute. Add the chicken broth, oyster sauce, shoyu, sugar, and vinegar, stirring to combine. Bring to a boil, then reduce the heat and simmer, stirring occasionally, until the sauce is reduced by one-third, about 10 minutes.

In a small bowl, whisk the cornstarch with 2 tablespoons water to form a smooth slurry, then stir into the sauce. Continue simmering and stirring until the sauce thickens into a gravy, another 1 to 2 minutes. Stir in the sesame oil and season with salt and white pepper to taste. Reduce the heat to low and keep warm while you fry the omelets.

recipe and ingredients continue →

Chinese food, especially what many people would consider Chinese American food, is my personal happy place. Growing up on Hilo, we had killer spots like Sun Sun Lau, Mun Cheong Lau, Cheng's, Leung's, Kow's, and New China—all of which you could depend on for a plate of crispy lemon chicken, wok-fried lo mein, savory black bean spareribs, and the local favorite, egg foo young. I'm not sure why, but Hawai'i has a particular appreciation for that last dish—maybe because it has gravy on top?

In terms of technique, most people approach egg foo young like cooking an omelet or frittata, which is fine, but for crispy patties with an airy texture, you'll want a bit more oil in the pan than you'd use for, say, scrambled eggs. I've found the best way to make egg foo young patties is to borrow a method I've seen used for chiles rellenos: whip the eggs whites before folding them into the batter. The step adds a few minutes of arm work but results in puffy, fluffy, and well-browned egg foo young that soaks up gravy like a dream. I've included both bean sprouts and celery because I like the different types of crunch they provide, but you can use one or the other. Likewise, shrimp can be substituted for any type of chopped leftover meat or tofu you have on hand.

Shrimp Egg Foo Young *continued*

For the omelets

6 large eggs

1 teaspoon cornstarch

½ teaspoon kosher salt, plus more as needed

½ pound peeled raw jumbo shrimp, halved lengthwise and roughly chopped

1 cup bean sprouts (about 2 ounces)

½ cup chopped celery (about 1 large stalk)

Chopped scallion greens (reserved from making the gravy)

Neutral oil, for shallow-frying

Cooked white rice, for serving

SERVES 4

Make the omelets: Separate the egg whites from the yolks into two bowls: the whites into a large bowl and the yolks into a small bowl. Using an electric hand mixer, beat the egg whites on medium speed just until stiff peaks form, about 4 minutes.

Add the cornstarch and salt to the small bowl with the egg yolks and whisk to combine, then pour the beaten yolks into the bowl with the egg whites and fold until just combined (some streaks are fine). Add the shrimp, bean sprouts, celery, and most of the scallion greens (set a tablespoon or so aside for garnish). Fold to combine.

Line a tray or plate with paper towels and have it near the stove. In a large skillet or wok, heat ½ inch of oil over medium-high heat until it begins to shimmer. Test the temperature by adding a dollop of the egg mixture. If it instantly sizzles when it hits the oil, you're ready to fry.

If you're using a 12-inch skillet, you should be able to cook two omelets at a time, or cook them individually in a smaller skillet or wok. Ladle about ¾ cup of the egg mixture into the skillet for each omelet. Cook, basting the top with hot oil, until the bottom sets and turns golden, 2 to 3 minutes.

Carefully flip using a spatula or tongs and cook, basting again with the oil, on the other side until cooked through, 1 to 2 minutes longer. Drain the omelets on the paper towels and season with a pinch of salt. Repeat with the remaining mixture, adding more oil if needed.

Serve immediately over rice, with gravy on top or on the side, garnished with the remaining scallions.

Seared Snapper
with Spicy-Sweet Fruit Curry

Neutral oil, for pan-frying

4 small red snapper fillets (about 4 ounces each)

Kosher salt and freshly ground black pepper

1 medium green apple, peeled, cored, and finely chopped

1 ripe peach or mango, peeled, pitted, and finely chopped

1 cup canned full-fat coconut milk

1 tablespoon Thai red curry paste

2 teaspoons fish sauce

2 teaspoons light brown sugar, plus more to taste

¼ cup finely chopped fresh basil leaves

Extra-virgin olive oil, for drizzling

Lime wedges, for squeezing

Cooked white rice, for serving

SERVES 2

Add just enough neutral oil to a large skillet to coat the bottom of the pan and set it over medium-high heat.

While the pan is heating, pat the fillets dry and season generously with salt and pepper on both sides. Once the oil in the pan is shimmering, add the fillets to the pan skin-side down, making sure there's enough space so they don't touch. Cook the fish, undisturbed, until seared and lightly browned, 3 to 4 minutes. Carefully flip and continue cooking for another 90 seconds to 2 minutes. The fish should end up medium-well: It will flake easily with a fork but is still soft and tender. Transfer to a plate.

With the skillet still over medium-high heat, drizzle in another coat of neutral oil. When the oil is shimmering, add the fruit and cook, stirring occasionally, until softened and tender, 4 to 5 minutes.

Stir in the coconut milk, curry paste, fish sauce, brown sugar, 2 tablespoons water, and a pinch of salt. Continue cooking until everything is incorporated, 1 to 2 minutes. Transfer the sauce to a tall heatproof jar and puree using an immersion blender. If the sauce is too thick to easily pour, add a few spoonfuls of water. Season to taste with more salt or brown sugar as needed.

Divide the curry sauce between two serving plates and top with the seared fish. Garnish with the basil, a drizzle of olive oil, and a squeeze of lime. Serve immediately with rice.

The inspiration for this recipe came from a now-closed restaurant in San Francisco called AL's Place (shout out to Aaron London), which had a Thai-leaning curry on the menu made with whatever stone fruit was in season. The nuanced natural sweetness of fruit balances the spice and salt to create a sauce that tastes elegant without too much work.

Once you've seared the fish, the curry sauce comes together in the same pan and is then blended into a smooth, rich, coconutty curry. I've given some suggestions, but there's a long list of fruits that will work here—stone fruit, of course, but also pineapple, berries, melon, pear, or grapes. Aim to use 2 to 2½ cups of finely chopped fruit and a combination of tart and sweet so the curry stays relatively balanced. There's no better flex for date night than picking up whatever ripe fruit is at the farmers market, turning it into a meal worthy of a fancy restaurant, and only having one pan to wash—and doing it in less than half an hour, at that.

PORK & BEEF

Bistek Bites

- 3 tablespoons shoyu (soy sauce)
- 1 tablespoon oyster sauce
- Grated zest and juice of 1 lemon
- 1 tablespoon sugar
- 1 pound rib-eye steak, cut into 1-inch cubes
- Kosher salt and freshly ground black pepper
- 1 tablespoon neutral oil
- 2 tablespoons butter
- 3 cloves garlic, smashed and peeled
- 1-inch piece fresh ginger, peeled and grated
- ½ medium red onion, sliced

SERVES 2

In a small bowl, whisk together the shoyu, oyster sauce, lemon juice, and sugar until the sugar is dissolved. Set aside. Season the steak pieces evenly with a few pinches of salt and pepper.

In a large sauté pan or cast-iron skillet, heat the oil over medium-high heat until it begins to shimmer and start to smoke.

Working in batches to avoid overcrowding, add the steak pieces to the pan and sear them, moving them as little as possible, until an even browned crust forms, about 2 minutes per side. Transfer the seared steak pieces to a plate.

Reduce the heat to medium and add the butter, garlic, and ginger to the empty pan. Cook, stirring and scraping up any browned bits from the bottom of the pan, until the garlic and ginger are softened and fragrant, 1 to 2 minutes. Add the shoyu mixture and continue cooking, stirring and scraping the bottom of the pan, until about half the liquid has reduced and the sauce begins to resemble a glaze, another 2 minutes.

Return the seared steak to the pan and add the onion, tossing to coat in the sauce. Remove from the heat. Transfer the steak pieces to a plate and garnish with the lemon zest before serving.

Bistek means "steak," but in the Filipino kitchen, it more specifically means steak seasoned with shoyu and citrus. And since both those ingredients are liquid, that also means bistek is often more of a braised steak than a seared one that you'd fry up in a skillet. But there is a way to get the best of both worlds: a flavorful sauce *and* a nice sear. This dish started out as a riff on garlic butter steak bites, which is a *pau hana* (happy hour) favorite you'll find at local bars. After cubing up a nice, marbled steak, the chunks are seared in a hot skillet to form a crust, with the flavorful bits left behind in the pan serving as the basis for a simple pan sauce made with shoyu, lemon, and butter. The finishing touch is tossing the steak with slivers of raw onion and lemon zest, which cut through the rich and fatty beef and bring the dish into focus. It's great eaten over rice for an easy dinner, but it's a wonderful bar snack, too—I like to spear the steak bites with a frilly toothpick for the full effect.

Longganisa Sliders

- 1 pound ground pork
- 10 cloves garlic, finely minced
- 6 tablespoons light brown sugar
- 1 tablespoon paprika
- 1 tablespoon cornstarch
- 2 teaspoons kosher salt
- 1 teaspoon freshly ground black pepper
- 1 teaspoon ground annatto (or ¾ teaspoon paprika + ¼ teaspoon ground turmeric)
- Neutral oil, for frying
- ½ cup banana ketchup or honey barbecue sauce
- 8 dinner rolls or sweet rolls, split
- 3 tablespoons mayonnaise
- ½ small white onion, thinly sliced into rings
- 8 dill pickle chips (the refrigerated kind)

MAKES 12 SLIDERS

In a large bowl, combine the pork, garlic, brown sugar, paprika, cornstarch, salt, pepper, and annatto. Using your hands, mix until well combined. Cover and refrigerate for at least 2 hours and up to overnight. Divide the longganisa into 12 equal portions and form into patties about the size of the top of a soda can.

Drizzle enough oil into a large skillet to lightly coat the bottom of the pan and set over medium-high heat. Once the oil is shimmering, working in batches to avoid overcrowding, add the longganisa patties and fry, turning them frequently, until lightly browned on the outside, 4 to 5 minutes total. During the last minute, baste each patty on both sides with banana ketchup, which should reduce and form a sticky glaze, then transfer to a plate.

Rinse out the skillet and give it a quick wipe before returning it to medium-high heat. Working in batches, brush the inside of each split roll with mayo and toast in the pan until browned, 2 to 3 minutes.

Top each roll with a longganisa patty, onion slices, and a dill pickle. Serve immediately.

These mini burgers filled with sweet, garlicky sausages are a riff on a dish my buddy Charles Olalia used to serve at his very fun and creative Filipino restaurant in Los Angeles, Ma'am Sir. Distinct for its signature red color thanks to ground annatto, longganisa is usually associated with breakfast, when it's eaten with eggs and garlic (aka longsilog). But that's just scratching the surface of its potential. There are many different styles of longganisa all over the Philippines, with some leaning more vinegary, or spicy, or cured in sausage casings. My favorite, though, is the simplest: the bold and direct style of longganisa from Central Luzon that's punched up with loads of pungent garlic, brown sugar, and black pepper, with paprika and annatto adding a mild earthy flavor and color. At home, I always make "skinless" longganisa, which is loose ground sausage and saves the work of stuffing the meat into casings.

At Ma'am Sir, the garlicky longganisa sliders were topped with atchara, a pickled papaya slaw, but I pushed the toppings for mine in a different direction, inspired by a certain seasonal rib sandwich from a well-known fast-food chain. As they fry in the skillet, brush the sausage patties with banana ketchup or barbecue sauce to create a sticky glaze, then top each slider with some pickle chips and raw onion, which add tang and sharpness that cuts through the rich sausage. As for buns, Hawaiian sweet rolls would be a fun touch, but any bread similar to Filipino pan de sal, such as dinner rolls or hoagie rolls cut in half, works well, too.

Pan-Fried Pork Chops
with Breakfast Ketchup

For the breakfast ketchup

½ cup ketchup, plus more to taste

¼ cup bourbon barrel–aged maple syrup or other real maple syrup, plus more to taste

For the pork chops

4 bone-in pork rib chops (about 7 ounces each), ¾ inch thick

2 teaspoons kosher salt

1 teaspoon garlic powder

1 teaspoon ground white pepper

Neutral oil, for frying

½ cup cornstarch

¼ cup all-purpose flour

SERVES 2 TO 4

Make the breakfast ketchup: In a small bowl, stir together the ketchup and maple syrup, adjusting the ratio to taste as desired. Set aside.

Cook the pork chops: Season the chops all over (including the fat cap) with salt, garlic powder, and white pepper. Aim for a ratio of two parts salt to one part garlic powder and white pepper.

Line a plate with paper towels and have it near the stove. Pour ½ inch oil into a large skillet and heat over medium-high heat until it reads 350°F on a thermometer.

While the oil is heating, combine the cornstarch and flour in a medium bowl.

Working in batches to avoid overcrowding, dredge the pork chops in the flour mixture, without shaking off any excess flour, and add to the pan. Fry the pork chops until they're golden brown and the meat is firm and slightly springy to the touch, about 5 minutes per side. Transfer to the paper towels.

When cool enough to handle, carve the meat from the bones and slice, against the grain, into 1-inch-wide pieces, saving the bones for gnawing. Serve immediately (the chops are best eaten warm) with the breakfast ketchup for dipping.

When it comes to bar pupus in Hawai'i, the crispy, pan-fried pork chop deserves to have its jersey hung in the rafters. Side Street Inn, a beloved restaurant with the spirit of a dive bar on O'ahu, serves the most famous version—crispy but a little oily, and heavy on rich porky flavor—but you'll usually find it on the menu at any place that will serve you a shot and a beer alongside boiled peanuts and shoyu wieners. I don't think I have to spend much time explaining the handshake that happens between a gnawing of a fried chop bone and a draft beer, but here we are. The two crucial elements of the pan-fried pork chop are the thickness and the dredge. I use the commonly found ¾-inch chop, as that thickness also allows you to develop a crispy golden-brown hue without the meat being overcooked. Using a mixture of cornstarch and flour creates a thin craggily crust that clings to the pork and browns up nicely in the pan.

You might be wondering, what's up with this dipping sauce though? Side Street serves theirs with regular ketchup, and we serve a riff on that at Tiffany's, with our improved sweet and tangy "breakfast ketchup." Somehow, our mixture of ketchup and syrup works amazingly well with the fatty chop seasoned with garlic powder and white pepper. I suggest investing in some nicer maple syrup, like the kind aged in bourbon barrels, which adds a touch of much-needed class.

"Pinoy BBQ" Oven Sticky Ribs

For the spice-rubbed ribs

1 full rack pork spareribs (about 2½ pounds)

4 teaspoons brown sugar

2 teaspoons kosher salt

2 teaspoons garlic powder

1 teaspoon freshly ground black pepper

For the barbecue sauce

½ cup banana ketchup

3 tablespoons oyster sauce

2 tablespoons honey

2 tablespoons shoyu (soy sauce)

2 tablespoons fresh orange juice

2 tablespoons apple cider vinegar

3 cloves garlic, minced or grated

½ teaspoon freshly ground black pepper

SERVES 2 TO 4

Preheat the oven to 275°F. Line a baking sheet with aluminum foil.

Prepare the ribs: If not already removed, peel off the membrane covering the bones on the back of the ribs. This helps the rub seasoning penetrate better. Carefully slide a paring knife under the membrane to loosen, then pull it off with your fingers (use a kitchen towel for a better grip).

In a small bowl, mix together the brown sugar, salt, garlic powder, and pepper. Rub the spice mixture evenly over both sides of the ribs.

Make the barbecue sauce: In a saucepan, combine the banana ketchup, oyster sauce, honey, shoyu, orange juice, vinegar, garlic, and pepper. Cook over medium heat, stirring occasionally, until the sauce is slightly thickened, 5 to 7 minutes. Remove from the heat.

Place the seasoned ribs on the baking sheet, meat-side up. Cover the ribs with another sheet of foil and seal the edges tightly to create a packet. Bake until the meat is tender and pulls away from the bone easily, 2 to 2½ hours.

Remove the ribs from the oven. Set the oven to broil at high heat (400°F) and move the oven rack to the highest position.

Carefully open the foil pouch to expose the ribs. Brush both sides generously with the barbecue sauce. Return the ribs to the oven, uncovered and with the meaty side up, and broil for 2 to 3 minutes, until slightly charred and crispy. Remove the ribs from the oven, add a final coat of sauce, and broil for another 2 to 3 minutes, until caramelized and sticky.

Let cool slightly before slicing into individual ribs and serving with any remaining barbecue sauce on the side.

The idea behind these ribs was to take the tangy-sweet sauce used for Filipino barbecue sticks and apply it to American ribs—the best of both worlds in my opinion, as long as you have some moist towelettes handy. I know there will be barbecue purists out there who turn their noses up at ribs cooked in the oven, but preparing them this way takes advantage of your broiler and uses the blast of heat to achieve a sticky caramelized glaze that will impress your friends and silence any haters. If you're committed to charcoal or gas, you can also parcook the wrapped ribs in the oven and finish them with the sauce on a high-heat grill.

Wok Pastor Tacos

For the al pastor

3 pounds boneless pork butt

¼ cup neutral oil

3 dried guajillo chiles, stemmed and seeded

2 dried ancho chiles, stemmed and seeded

½ medium white onion, cut into wedges

3 cloves garlic, peeled but whole

½ medium pineapple, cored, peeled, and cut into ¼-inch chunks

¼ cup apple cider vinegar

1 tablespoon achiote paste

2 teaspoons kosher salt

1 teaspoon ground cumin

1 teaspoon dried oregano

½ teaspoon ground cinnamon

¼ teaspoon ground allspice

Make the al pastor: Cut the pork into ½-inch chunks by first slicing the pork butt into steaks, then into long slices, then into cubes. Place the pork in a large bowl, cover, and set aside.

In a wok or large skillet, heat the oil over medium-high heat until it begins to shimmer. Add the dried chiles, onion, and garlic and stir-fry until the chiles soften and become fragrant, about 3 minutes. Remove the pan from the heat, then use a slotted spoon to transfer the chiles, onion, and garlic to a blender. Reserve the oil.

Add half of the pineapple, the vinegar, achiote paste, salt, cumin, oregano, cinnamon, and allspice to the blender. Blend on low speed until a smooth sauce forms. With the machine running, slowly pour in the reserved oil and blend until totally incorporated.

Pour the pastor marinade over the pork and stir to combine. Let rest at room temperature (see Note) while you prepare the salsa.

recipe and ingredients continue →

This recipe started out as a family meal request at the restaurant: The kitchen wanted al pastor tacos. Perhaps you've had a similar situation with your crews and, like me, didn't have a rotisserie spit to make this dish the traditional way. But after getting creative, I've learned all you need to make an excellent al pastor cheat is a big wok.

Traditional al pastor—which actually traces its roots to a Lebanese dish by way of Mexico—is made by marinating cuts of pork in seasoned chile paste, then roasting them on a spit. But stir-frying the pork *in* the marinade achieves 90 percent of the effect with far less hassle: The pork absorbs the sauce as it cooks, saving on marinating time, and once the liquid has evaporated, the sauce sears and caramelizes on the pan, which creates a smoky, slightly sweet crust that stands in for what you would get from flame-roasting. A wok is best for the technique, since it will give you ample room to stir the meat at high heat, but a big skillet or Dutch oven with high sides can also work, if that's what you have.

I've also included a recipe for a basic avocado salsa, made without tomatillos (which can be hard to find on Maui). And, depending on your access to high-quality corn tortillas (mine is limited), you might want to double-tortilla your tacos to limit breakage. One thing we don't lack in Hawai'i, though, is pineapple. Use the fresh kind here if you can—even your average supermarket pineapple is better than the canned stuff in this case, as the enzymes in the fresh fruit are more effective at tenderizing the pork, even during their very brief marination time.

Note: Avoid marinating the pork longer than 1 hour or it will go from being tender to mushy. If you'd like to make this dish in advance, prepare the marinade separately and store in the fridge for up to a day before combining with the meat.

For the avocado salsa

2 tablespoons neutral oil

½ medium white onion, roughly chopped

2 jalapeños, stemmed and seeded

2 large avocados, halved and pitted

½ small bunch of cilantro (about 15 sprigs)

¼ cup fresh lime juice (from 2 large limes)

1 teaspoon kosher salt, plus more to taste

For assembly

Neutral oil, for frying

24 corn tortillas, heated and kept warm (or 48, if you prefer double tortillas)

½ cup finely chopped fresh cilantro

1 medium red onion, finely diced

4 limes, cut into eighths

MAKES 24 TACOS; SERVES 8

Make the avocado salsa: Wipe out the same wok or large skillet you used for the marinade. Place over medium heat, add the oil, and heat until shimmering. Add the onion and jalapeños and cook, stirring occasionally, until the onion and chiles have softened, about 5 minutes.

Remove the pan from the heat and let cool slightly before transferring the onion and chiles to a blender or food processor. Scoop the avocado flesh into the blender and add the cilantro, lime juice, and salt and blend until smooth. Taste and season with more salt, thinning out the salsa with splashes of cold water if needed (you want a spoonable consistency). Refrigerate until ready to serve.

To assemble: After the pork has marinated for 15 minutes or so, place the same wok or large skillet over medium-high heat and drizzle with a light coat of oil. Once the oil begins to smoke, add about one-third of the marinated pork mixture and cook, stirring often, until the pork is cooked through and slightly browned and charred at the edges, and the sauce has reduced, about 5 minutes. Transfer the cooked meat to a serving platter or bowl. Repeat with the remaining pork, adding a drizzle of oil between batches as needed.

Drizzle the wok with another light coat of oil and add the remaining pineapple, cooking while stirring often for 2 to 3 minutes, until warmed through and slightly softened. Place the seared pineapple over the pork.

Serve the meat and pineapple immediately with warmed tortillas, the avocado salsa, cilantro, diced onions, and lime wedges.

SOSICK
ALOHA STATE
10 24
4WD

Lechon Liempo

2 tablespoons plus 2 teaspoons kosher salt

1 tablespoon freshly ground black pepper

1 tablespoon paprika

1 tablespoon chili powder

1 tablespoon light brown sugar

2 teaspoons garlic powder

2 teaspoons onion powder

1 whole skin-on pork belly (about 6 pounds)

⅓ cup apple cider vinegar

2 tablespoons shoyu (soy sauce)

1 cup chopped garlic (about 4 whole heads)

1 cup chopped scallions

1 cup chopped red onions

1 teaspoon baking powder

Special equipment: butcher's or cooking twine

SERVES 8 TO 12

In a small bowl, mix together the 2 tablespoons salt, the pepper, paprika, chili powder, brown sugar, garlic powder, and onion powder until combined.

Place the pork belly skin-side up on a clean, flat surface. Use the tip of a sharp knife to poke through the skin all over, which will help the fat render and will baste the pork. Flip the belly over and score the flesh deeply with the sharp knife cut at an angle using strokes about 1 inch apart. Rotate the knife 90 degrees and repeat to create a diamond pattern.

Rub the meat side with the vinegar and shoyu. Sprinkle the seasoning mixture over the meat side of the pork belly, pressing to help it stick. Spread the chopped garlic, scallions, and red onions evenly over the surface.

Starting from one end, roll the pork belly tightly to form a roll (if one end is longer than the other, start rolling on that end). Use butcher's twine to tie the rolled pork belly securely every 2 inches or so along its length. Combine the remaining 2 teaspoons salt with the baking powder and rub evenly over the surface of the pork roll. Wrap tightly in plastic and refrigerate for at least 6 hours, or up to 3 days.

When ready to cook, preheat the oven to 300°F.

Place the rolled and tied pork belly on a rack in a roasting pan. Roast until a meat thermometer inserted into the center registers 160°F, 2 to 3 hours, basting with the pan drippings every 30 minutes.

Remove the pork belly from the oven and cover with foil. Increase the oven temperature to 500°F. Once the oven is heated, remove the foil and return the pork to the oven, roasting until the skin is completely crisp and blistered, another 20 to 30 minutes. (If you're not ready to serve immediately, the foil-covered pork belly can rest for up to 2 hours before finishing.)

Let the pork belly rest for 5 to 10 minutes before cutting into ½-inch slices and serving.

I'll be up front with you: This oven-roasted Filipino pork belly is one of the more involved recipes in the book, both in terms of getting your hands on the star ingredient and the advance preparation. That said, when you nail it, lechon is a magnificent centerpiece worthy of the most special feast.

The best place to find a whole skin-on pork belly is usually an Asian supermarket, but you might also have luck asking your local specialty butcher.

If you've had lechon before, you know that one of the best parts is the crispy, bubbly skin. But often the actual meat doesn't get as much attention. My solution to this problem came from my time spent in Charleston, South Carolina, where whole-hog barbecue is practically a religion: Create a BBQ-style dry rub to massage over the inside of the pork belly roll while the outside skin crisps up.

Ground Beef Galbi Bowls

½ cup unsweetened applesauce

¼ cup shoyu (soy sauce)

3 tablespoons brown sugar

1 tablespoon apple cider vinegar

2 teaspoons toasted sesame oil

1 teaspoon gochugaru (Korean chile flakes) or red chile flakes

¼ teaspoon freshly ground black pepper

1 tablespoon neutral oil

2 scallions, thinly sliced, white and green parts kept separate

4 cloves garlic, minced or grated

1 pound ground beef (85/15)

1 teaspoon toasted sesame seeds

For serving

Cooked white rice or large lettuce leaves

Broccoli Banchan (page 91)

Spicy Garlic Cucumbers (page 92)

White Kimchi (page 252) or store-bought kimchi

SERVES 4

In a small bowl, whisk together the applesauce, shoyu, brown sugar, vinegar, sesame oil, gochugaru, and black pepper. Set aside.

In a large skillet, heat the neutral oil over medium-high heat until shimmering. Add the scallion whites and the garlic and cook, stirring constantly, until fragrant, about 1 minute. Add the ground beef and cook until browned, 3 to 5 minutes, using a spatula to crumble the beef as it cooks.

Stir in the shoyu mixture and simmer until most of the liquid has evaporated and a sauce has formed, 3 to 4 minutes. Remove the pan from the heat and top with the scallion greens and sesame seeds.

Serve over white rice with any combination of broccoli banchan, spicy garlic cucumbers, and kimchi.

I've tried to include a surplus of quick weeknight dinners in this book, but this one might be the quickest of them all: a shortcut version of Korean galbi made with ground beef that comes together in less than 20 minutes. Pair it with one or two of the banchan suggested above, either over a rice bowl or folded into a low-carb lettuce wrap, and your meal is set. It's become a major favorite on nights when Janice and I get back from our workout class starving. You'll only need to wash one pan, too.

Diner Burgers
with Smoky Tomato Mayo

1 large seedless cucumber, thinly sliced

¼ large sweet onion, thinly sliced

2 tablespoons sugar

2 teaspoons kosher salt

2 tablespoons apple cider vinegar

1 tablespoon distilled white vinegar

⅓ cup ketchup

2 tablespoons tomato paste

1½ pounds ground beef (80/20)

4 soft hamburger buns, split

⅓ cup mayonnaise, plus more for the buns

Garlic salt

Freshly ground black pepper

4 slices yellow American cheese

SERVES 4

In a medium bowl, toss the cucumber and onion with the sugar and salt, then transfer to the fridge. Refrigerate for 15 minutes.

After 15 minutes, drain the liquid from the cucumber mixture and add both vinegars, tossing to combine. Return to the fridge and chill while you form the burgers. (You can also do this step the day before and refrigerate the pickles overnight.)

In a small bowl, stir together the ketchup and tomato paste until combined. Set aside.

Divide the ground beef into 4 equal portions and use your hands or the lid from a plastic container to shape each one into a patty 1 inch thick, taking care not to overwork the meat.

Heat a 12-inch skillet over medium-high heat. When the pan is heated (it should feel very warm when you hold your hand over it), brush each half of the hamburger buns with mayo, then place them in the pan mayo-side down, working in batches if necessary. Toast the buns for about 1 minute, until golden brown. Repeat with the remaining buns, then set aside. Brush out any crumbs from the pan and return the skillet to medium-high heat.

recipe continues →

I enjoy a simple burger, but when you're doing something simple, it's important that each element you add makes a strong contribution. That's the philosophy behind this burger, which won us the second-place award at an impromptu burger cook-off at a food festival I was invited to in Los Angeles several years ago. My kitchen crew at the time and I had flown out from Maui to cook at this event, and we had a big night out in Koreatown the night before (the same night where I ate some incredible galbijjim, as described on page 219). We all showed up the next day hungover, the last team to arrive, and pulled together our planned burger made with condiments that we had hauled there in our carry-ons.

The idea was to take a basic cheeseburger with pickles, ketchup, and mayo and amplify it. We mixed together tomato paste with ketchup and essentially seared/fried it in a hot pan, which gave it a slightly smoky flavor and concentrated the tomatoey flavors—umami-boosted ketchup, essentially, that we mixed with mayo. We also made some snappy sweet pickles and then were off to the races smashing and serving a few hundred burgers behind a hot griddle.

The burger was a big hit, and although I was runner-up in the contest (if you followed me on *Top Chef,* you might sense a theme), it was good enough that celebrity judges Seth Rogen and Tiffani Thiessen both posted about it on their social media. I'll take whatever victory I can get! Plus, the fact that I can now share this burger with you here, in my book, is the real prize.

When the skillet starts to smoke, sprinkle the patties generously with garlic salt and pepper on one side. Place them seasoned-side down in the skillet, spacing them out as much as possible and smashing them down firmly with a spatula (you might need to work in batches, depending on the size of your skillet). Cook the burgers until they're well seared and browned on the bottom, 3 to 4 minutes. Season the other side of the patties with garlic salt and pepper, then use a spatula to flip the patties and cook until they reach your desired internal temperature. I like mine medium to medium-well, which takes another 3 to 4 minutes.

Once you've flipped the burgers, add a slice of cheese to each. The residual heat should melt the cheese before the second side is finished cooking, but you can also cover the pan with a lid to speed up the melting. Transfer the cooked patties to a plate and loosely cover to keep warm.

Use a paper towel to brush out any burned bits from the skillet you cooked the burgers in, but don't worry about wiping it clean. Increase the heat to high, add the ketchup-tomato paste mixture, and cook, stirring constantly, until it sizzles, reduces, and becomes a thick, darkened paste, 2 to 3 minutes. Remove the pan from the heat and scrape the mixture back into the small bowl. Let cool for a few minutes, then stir in the ⅓ cup mayo.

Remove the pickles from the fridge. Place the patties on the bottom buns, top with pickles, and dollop a generous amount of the tomato mayo on the top buns. Serve immediately.

Caramelized Kimchi Loco Moco

For the burgers

1 pound ground beef (85/15)

½ cup finely minced sweet onion

¼ cup panko bread crumbs

4 ounces Spam, finely diced

2 tablespoons mayonnaise

1 teaspoon garlic salt

½ teaspoon freshly ground black pepper

1 large egg

1 tablespoon neutral oil

For the kimchi gravy and eggs

Neutral oil, as needed

1 cup roughly chopped kimchi, with juices

3 tablespoons butter

1 tablespoon shoyu (soy sauce), plus more to taste

2 tablespoons all-purpose flour

2 cups reduced-sodium beef stock

4 large eggs

Garlic salt

Freshly ground black pepper

Make the burgers: In a large bowl, combine the ground beef, onion, panko, Spam, mayo, garlic salt, pepper, and egg. Mix until everything is just combined. Divide the mixture into 4 roughly equal portions, then use your hands to shape them into patties about ½ inch thick.

Preheat the oven to 425°F. Place a sheet pan on the middle rack to heat while the oven is warming.

In a large skillet, heat the oil over medium-high heat until it starts to shimmer. Carefully place the patties in the pan, spacing them out evenly (you can also cook them in batches if needed). Pan-fry until the patties are browned on the outside and cooked through in the middle, 4 to 5 minutes per side. Transfer the patties to a clean plate to rest.

Make the kimchi gravy: Without wiping out the skillet, drizzle in enough oil to lightly coat the bottom of the pan. Once the oil begins to shimmer, add the chopped kimchi and cook, stirring, until most of the liquid from the kimchi has evaporated, 2 to 3 minutes. Add the butter and shoyu, and reduce the heat to medium.

recipe and ingredients continue →

If you're reading this book, you might already know what loco moco is. If not, know that it features at least one burger patty, rice, gravy, and fried eggs, that it was invented in Hilo, and that it almost always requires a nap after finishing. Along with the classic loco moco, restaurants here serve it in all kinds of variations—katsu moco, char siu moco, teriyaki moco, you name it. This is my contribution to the canon: loco moco topped with a tangy rich gravy enhanced with caramelized kimchi. The same way that the Korean stew kimchi jjigae is best made with older, well-fermented kimchi that breaks down in the broth, slowly caramelizing kimchi in butter creates the base for a smooth kimchi gravy with a deep and complex flavor. (The takeaway here is never buy a small jar of kimchi, because there are always ways to use old kimchi.)

When my relatives who now live on the mainland visit, their kids always ask for loco moco. And when I am making a batch for them (or anyone), I'm throwing finely diced Spam in with the meat. There's nothing like seasoning ground beef with bits of salted cured meat, which counterintuitively makes the patties lighter and fluffier. If I'm cooking for a big crowd or pressed for time, I'll use frozen burger patties in a pinch, so feel free to make that swap if needed.

For serving

4 cups cooked rice

Chopped scallions

Tabasco sauce (optional)

SERVES 4

Continue cooking the kimchi until it starts to caramelize and brown around the edges, 3 to 4 minutes. Add the flour and stir to combine, cooking for about 30 seconds until no dry clumps of flour remain. Add the beef stock and season with more shoyu to taste. Simmer uncovered for 5 to 7 minutes to let the gravy thicken and the flavors meld.

Cook the eggs: While the gravy is simmering, carefully remove the hot sheet pan from the oven and drizzle with a coat of neutral oil to prevent sticking. Working quickly, crack the remaining 4 eggs onto the sheet pan, then return the pan to the oven and bake until the whites are set but the yolks are still runny, about 5 minutes. Remove from the oven and season with garlic salt and pepper.

To serve: Place 1 cup cooked rice on each plate and top with a patty, spoon over the gravy, then top with a fried egg, some chopped scallions, and a few shakes of Tabasco (if using). Serve immediately.

TACOS

Black Pepper Tri-Tip Donburi

For the black pepper tri-tip

2½-pound well-marbled tri-tip roast

½ cup shoyu (soy sauce)

½ teaspoon freshly ground black pepper

Neutral oil, for searing

For the wasabi cream

½ cup mayonnaise

4 teaspoons fresh lemon juice

4 teaspoons prepared wasabi

Kosher salt

For the sweet onion sauce

½ medium sweet onion, grated

3 tablespoons oyster sauce

2 tablespoons sugar

2 teaspoons shoyu (soy sauce)

2 teaspoons Worcestershire sauce

For assembly

4 to 6 cups cooked white rice

Shredded nori (optional)

Freshly ground black pepper

Fresh watercress or upland cress, stemmed

Raw egg yolks (optional)

SERVES 4 TO 6

Preheat the oven to 250°F.

Place the tri-tip in a resealable bag with the shoyu and black pepper, mixing everything well to coat. Let marinate at room temperature for at least 20 minutes and up to 1 hour.

Meanwhile, make the wasabi cream: In a small bowl, whisk together the mayo, lemon juice, wasabi, and a pinch of salt. Cover and set aside.

Transfer the tri-trip to a sheet pan and place it in the oven. Slow-roast until a meat thermometer inserted at the thickest point registers 125°F (for medium-rare), 30 to 40 minutes.

Remove the meat from the oven and let rest while you heat the skillet.

In a large skillet over medium-high heat, drizzle in enough oil to coat the bottom of the pan. Once the oil begins to smoke, add the tri-tip and sear for 2 to 3 minutes on each side, until a dark brown crust forms. Place the roast on a plate or cutting board and let rest. Do not wipe out the pan.

Make the sweet onion sauce: Place the skillet used to sear the roast over medium heat. Add the grated onion, stirring and scraping up any bits stuck to the bottom of the pan. Cook until the onions have softened and just begin to brown at the edges, about 6 minutes.

Deglaze the pan with ¼ cup water, the oyster sauce, sugar, shoyu, and Worcestershire sauce, scraping any stuck-on bits from the pan. Continue cooking, stirring often, until a spoonable sauce forms, 2 to 3 minutes. Remove from the heat.

Using a sharp knife, slice the rested tri-tip against the grain into thin slices.

To assemble the bowls: Place 1 cup of rice at the bottom of each bowl and cover with shredded nori (if using). Add a layer of sliced beef, then drizzle with the onion sauce and the wasabi cream and top with a big pinch of pepper. Arrange a small pile of watercress to one side of the bowl, then garnish with a raw egg yolk (if using). Serve immediately.

I love a good Japanese steak donburi, a rice bowl dish that you'll often see topped with marbled cuts of beef, like wagyu. But while anyone can make wagyu taste delicious, getting the same excitement from a more economical cut (in this case, tri-tip) is my idea of a fun challenge.

When cooking a tri-tip roast, I go with a classic reverse sear. The brief marinade in shoyu and black pepper not only adds flavor, but helps form a nice, caramelized crust once you sear the tri-tip.

I like dressing the beef up with two opposing sauces, Arby's style—one sharp and creamy, the other sweet and savory. From there, you can add on peppery watercress and a raw egg yolk to achieve the deluxe Japanese steakhouse effect.

Beef Pares

- 2 tablespoons neutral oil
- 1 medium yellow onion, sliced
- 4 scallions, finely chopped, white and green parts kept separate
- 2-inch piece fresh ginger, sliced and crushed with the butt of a knife
- 8 cloves garlic, minced
- 2 pounds beef chuck roast, brisket, or shank, cut into 1½-inch chunks
- 2 teaspoons beef bouillon powder
- 2 star anise or ½ teaspoon whole cloves
- 2 cinnamon sticks
- 2 teaspoons black peppercorns
- 3 bay leaves
- 6 tablespoons shoyu (soy sauce), plus more to taste
- 3 tablespoons oyster sauce
- 3 tablespoons light brown sugar, plus more to taste
- 2 tablespoons cornstarch
- Freshly ground black pepper

For serving

- Toasted Coconut Grits (page 124) or Triple-Garlic Rice (page 122)
- Sliced red onion (optional)
- Fried Garlic (optional; page 30)

SERVES 6

In a large pot or Dutch oven, heat the oil over medium-high heat until shimmering. Add the onion, scallion whites, ginger, and garlic and cook, stirring often, until fragrant, 1 to 2 minutes. Add the beef cubes and cook, stirring, until the beef is lightly browned all over, about 5 minutes total.

Stir in the beef bouillon powder, star anise, cinnamon sticks, peppercorns, and bay leaves, stirring just until the spices are fragrant, less than a minute. Stir in the shoyu, oyster sauce, brown sugar, and 2 cups water. Bring to a boil, then reduce the heat, cover, and simmer until the beef is very tender, 1½ to 2 hours.

In a small bowl, mix the cornstarch with 2 tablespoons water to make a slurry. Add the slurry to the beef mixture, stirring until the sauce thickens, 1 to 2 minutes. Taste and adjust the seasoning with shoyu, brown sugar, and black pepper if needed. Discard the cinnamon sticks and bay leaves.

To serve: Spoon the beef pares over a bowl of coconut grits or garlic rice, then garnish with the scallion greens and red onions and fried garlic, if desired.

This dish is a favorite of Nolan Gonzales, my longtime chef de cuisine at Tiffany's and my right-hand guy for over a decade, who's cooked with me at every restaurant I've opened. Nolan started working with me straight out of high school and he's been a huge part of our family's life and a major influence on the food we do. In fact, most of the R&D and specials at the restaurants run through him, and that includes a lot of the recipes in this book.

Nolan spent most of his childhood in the Philippines, and though we share a similar palate, I appreciate that he knows a lot of the dishes and flavors that I didn't grow up with, like this one. Beef pares is popular in the metro Manila area, and to me it represents the unfussy comfort of braised meat stewed down with cloves and peppercorns. Beef pares is traditionally served with plain rice or garlic rice, which are both perfect in their own way, but I think the dish's salty-sweet seasoning is fun to pair with savory coconut grits, which are amped up with toasted coconut flakes and creamy coconut milk.

Oven Galbijjim

4 pounds boneless short ribs (see Note), cut into 2-inch chunks

2 teaspoons kosher salt, plus more to taste

2 medium Korean (Asian) pears or large sweet apples, peeled, cored, and roughly chopped

1¼ cups mirin

1¼ cups shoyu (soy sauce)

¼ cup packed light brown sugar

2 teaspoons freshly ground black pepper, plus more to taste

1-inch piece fresh ginger, peeled and roughly chopped

12 cloves garlic, peeled but whole

2 tablespoons neutral oil

1 medium yellow onion, roughly chopped

1½ pounds fingerling potatoes

2 large carrots, peeled and cut into 1-inch chunks

1 tablespoon toasted sesame oil

Scallion Rice (page 123), for serving

Kimchi, homemade (page 252) or store-bought, for serving

SERVES 8

Season the meat on all sides with the salt and set aside.

In a blender, combine the pears, mirin, shoyu, brown sugar, black pepper, ginger, and 2 cloves of the garlic. Blend until smooth and set aside.

Preheat the oven to 350°F.

In a large Dutch oven or other ovenproof pot, heat the oil over medium-high heat until shimmering. Working in batches to avoid overcrowding, brown the beef chunks for about 2 minutes per side. Transfer the meat to a plate and set aside.

Add the remaining 10 cloves of garlic to the pot and cook, stirring often, until browned but not burned, 2 to 3 minutes. Pour the reserved pear mixture into the pot and bring the mixture to a boil.

Once boiling, remove the pot from the heat and return the short ribs to the pot along with the onion. The liquid should come three-quarters of the way up the short ribs; if not, add water as needed. Cover the pot tightly with aluminum foil and a tight-fitting lid, if you have one. Place the pot in the oven.

recipe continues →

Galbi is everywhere in Hawai'i, but galbijjim is not. Both of these Korean dishes involve short ribs seasoned with shoyu, sugar, and sesame oil (among other ingredients), but whereas galbi uses grilled, thin-cut marinated short ribs, galbijjim is a hearty stew of thick-cut short ribs. The first time I ever tried galbijjim was in Los Angeles, at a 24-hour spot called Sun Nong Dan, and I was instantly obsessed. Imagine a giant cauldron of braised beef so tender that it jiggles, topped with a layer of mozzarella that the waiter melts tableside with a blowtorch.

What makes an outstanding galbijjim is striking the right balance of salty and sweet. A mixture of mirin, brown sugar, and pear adds a mellow sweetness that balances the shoyu.

Traditionally galbijjim is simmered on the stovetop until the beef is tender, but I prefer to start the stew on the stove, then finish it in the oven, which helps the meat cook more evenly. The last step is to pull the cooked meat and vegetables from the pot and reduce the savory sauce left behind until it's a thick gravy, then toss the rested short ribs back in before serving. If you feel the need to add a layer of molten mozzarella on top, by all means, go ahead, but I'll save it for the next time I'm in LA.

Note: I use boneless short ribs, which is actually just trimmed sections of chuck roast and comes from the shoulder section of the cow rather than the ribs. Boneless short ribs tend to be much cheaper than bone-in short ribs, quicker cooking, and in my opinion, just as flavorful. If you're not able to find them, the best substitute is to buy a whole chuck roast, trim off as much fat as possible, and cut it into 2-inch chunks.

Bake the short ribs for 1½ hours. Remove from the oven and stir in the potatoes and carrots. Return to the oven and cook until the meat is fork-tender and the vegetables can be pierced easily, another 45 minutes to 1 hour.

Remove the pot from the oven and transfer the beef and vegetables to a plate, then cover and set aside. Use a ladle to skim off as much fat from the stew as you like, then place the pot over medium-high heat and bring to a boil once more. Continue cooking, stirring often, until the sauce is reduced by half and has a gravy-like consistency, about 10 minutes. Season to taste with salt and pepper.

Once the sauce is thickened, remove the pot from the heat and stir in the reserved short ribs and vegetables and the sesame oil. Serve with scallion rice and kimchi.

SALVAGE
PUBLIC
HONOLULU

Prime Rib Roast
with Shoyu Jus

2 tablespoons kosher salt

2 tablespoons freshly ground black pepper

5- to 7-pound bone-in prime rib roast

For serving

Shoyu Jus (recipe follows)

Ginger Chimichurri (page 259)

Double Hot Horseradish Mustard (page 260)

Boursin Mashed Potatoes (page 86)

SERVES 12

In a small bowl, combine the salt and pepper. Pat the roast dry with paper towels. Rub the salt and pepper mixture evenly all over the rib roast and cover tightly with plastic wrap. Place in the fridge for at least 2 hours and up to 2 days (overnight is a great middle ground).

About an hour before you start cooking, remove the roast from the fridge and let it come to room temperature. Preheat the oven to 250°F.

Set the rib roast on a roasting pan fat-side up (you don't need a roasting rack) and place, uncovered, in the oven. Cook for 25 to 30 minutes per pound, or until a meat thermometer inserted in the thickest section registers 130°F (for medium-rare).

Remove the rib roast from the oven and cover tightly with foil (you can remove the beef drippings at this point to make the jus, if desired). Let rest for at least 30 minutes, up to 1 hour.

Increase the oven temperature to 500°F.

Remove the foil, place the roast back in the heated oven, and cook until the crust is browned and crispy, 6 to 8 minutes. Remove from the oven.

To serve: Carve the roast and serve with shoyu jus, ginger chimichurri, and double hot horseradish mustard for topping, and Boursin mashed potatoes on the side.

recipe continues →

Forget presents. Forget decorations. The pinnacle of the holidays for me is a slab of medium-rare beef. And nothing scratches that itch like a classically prepared prime rib. My philosophy is simple: Splurge on prime-grade beef (as opposed to choice or select), season it very simply, roast it slowly, finish it on high heat to form a crust, and focus any creative energy on making fun condiments. I like to go with three different options so there's something for everyone: a traditional beef dripping au jus flavored with shoyu, a bright herb chimichurri punched up with ginger, and a creamy horseradish and Chinese hot mustard sauce. Perfection.

Shoyu Jus MAKES ABOUT 2 CUPS

- ¼ cup beef drippings or butter
- ½ cup dry red wine (whatever you have on hand is fine)
- 2 cups low-sodium beef broth
- 1 teaspoon light brown sugar
- 1 tablespoon shoyu (soy sauce), plus more to taste
- 1 teaspoon Worcestershire sauce
- ¼ teaspoon freshly ground black pepper, plus more to taste

In a medium saucepan, melt the beef drippings or butter over medium heat, straining the drippings if needed for a clearer sauce. Add the red wine and reduce down to a syrup, about 5 minutes. Add the beef broth, brown sugar, shoyu, Worcestershire sauce, and black pepper. Bring the mixture to a boil, then reduce the heat to a simmer and cook, stirring occasionally, until reduced by a quarter or so and slightly thickened, another 10 to 15 minutes.

Taste and season with more shoyu or black pepper as needed. Once the flavors have melded, remove from the heat.

My older brother, Jeremy—also a chef—with his wife, Allison, and their kids, Joshua and Madison

DESSERTS & DRINKS

Rainbow Sherbet "Finger Jelly"

3 (6-ounce) boxes Jell-O, one each raspberry, orange, and lime

6 (¼-ounce) envelopes unflavored gelatin powder

1½ cups heavy cream

SERVES 8 TO 12

In a heatproof medium bowl, whisk together the box of raspberry Jell-O with 2 packets of gelatin. Bring 2 cups water to a boil, then add to the bowl, whisking until the powder is dissolved. Stir in ½ cup cold water, then ½ cup of the heavy cream. Pour the mixture into a 9 × 13-inch baking dish. Place in the fridge to set, 30 to 45 minutes.

Once the raspberry Jell-O is firm (and separated into two layers), repeat the same exact process again with the orange Jell-O, 2 envelopes of gelatin, and heavy cream, pouring that mixture on top of the chilled raspberry Jell-O and placing the dish back in the fridge.

Finally, once the orange layer is firm, repeat the process with the lime Jell-O and the remaining gelatin and heavy cream, pouring the mixture on top of the chilled orange Jell-O to create three colored layers. Chill again until the top layer is firm.

Cut into squares and serve cold.

Rainbow gelatin is a showstopper dessert at family get-togethers, potlucks, and all kinds of gatherings in Hawaiʻi. Kids and adults alike go crazy for it, and you'll often hear it called "finger Jell-O" because the sweet, fruity, jiggly cubes are a perfect finger food that puts a smile on everyone's face.

It's not difficult to make rainbow gelatin, but it can be time-consuming. That's because each layer of gelatin needs to fully set before the next one is poured on top, otherwise you'll end up with muddled layers. And for people who like to layer five, six, or even seven different flavors, all that cooling and setting time adds up.

Don't let that scare you away, however, because there is a somewhat magical "trick" that my coauthor learned from his mother-in-law that actually cuts the preparation time in half, and creates a more delicious, creamy dessert that holds its shape even in hot weather. Most layered gelatin recipes use sweetened condensed milk as one of the layers, but the lower-maintenance secret here is to swap in heavy cream instead. Simply mix the cream into the boiling water and gelatin packet and stir them together like normal, then pour everything into a baking pan. The fat in the cream will cause that layer to rise as it cools, self-separating the gelatin into two layers, one creamy and one clear. Once that layer is chilled, you can repeat the process as many times as you'd like with different flavors, adding two layers at a time and creating a cool ombre effect. Make sure to use heavy whipping cream here, as half-and-half and whole milk don't have enough fat content to cleanly separate.

I've gone with the classic rainbow sherbet flavor combo here of raspberry, orange, and lime, which perfectly complements the cream, but you can get as creative as you like with both the order of colors and the flavors.

Mandarin Microwave Mochi

- Cooking spray or neutral oil
- 1 (3-ounce) box orange Jell-O
- ½ cup boiling water
- 1 cup mochiko (glutinous rice flour)
- ½ cup pulp-free orange juice
- ⅓ cup sugar
- 1 teaspoon vanilla extract
- Distilled white vinegar (to keep the mochi pliable)
- Cornstarch or potato starch, for dusting
- 6 small mandarin oranges, peeled, rinsed, and dried
- Mint leaves (optional), for garnish

MAKES 6 MOCHI

Coat an 8 × 8-inch microwave-safe baking dish or microwave-safe bowl with cooking spray, or wipe with an oil-soaked paper towel.

In a heatproof medium bowl, whisk together the Jell-O with the boiling water until dissolved. Add the mochiko, orange juice, sugar, vanilla, and a few drops of vinegar, stirring until a smooth batter forms. Pour into the oil-coated dish and cover with plastic wrap.

Microwave on high for 2 minutes, then knead and fold the mochi with a silicone spatula. Cover with the plastic wrap and continue microwaving on high in 1-minute increments, kneading and folding each time, until the mochi dough is translucent, 4 to 5 minutes total. Uncover and let cool for about 10 minutes.

recipe continues →

Soft, sticky mochi that you can make in 15 minutes from start to finish? Seems like there must be a catch. And there is—it's called a microwave. The traditional way of making mochi involves lots of pounding and steaming, but modern conveniences have given us a tool that makes our lives easier, and we should take advantage, especially when it comes to making fresh mochi. One of my favorite things about this recipe—which is an old Hawai'i housewife standby—is that it's almost as easy to make as a batch of play dough, except way more fun for kids because they get to eat it afterward. Warm mochi is fairly easy to shape, so after the microwaved mochi is cool enough to handle, dust a work surface with cornstarch and have the kids roll and press the mochi into shapes.

The components are sweet rice flour (also known as mochiko, or glutinous rice flour), boiling water, the flavorings (orange gelatin mix, orange juice, vanilla, and sugar), and a little vinegar, which thins out the dough slightly so it stays pliable. The other requirement is a microwave-safe container for cooking the mochi. The glass baking dish you have on hand will work, but the best results will come from a pan-size silicone baking mold, since you can easily peel the mochi from the flexible shell.

You can use any flavor of gelatin you'd like, just know that some colors turn out more pleasant-looking than others (grape will end up more of a gray color). If you have any older kids who are feeling creative, fruit-filled mochi is a fun twist, too. Inspired by the famous Two Ladies Kitchen in Hilo, which makes fresh mochi every morning stuffed with various fresh fruits, a particularly cute combination is wrapping a small mandarin in orange-flavored mochi, then decorating it with a small mint leaf stem. Once you've mastered that, give strawberries a try.

Mandarin Microwave Mochi *continued*

When the mochi is cool enough to handle but still warm enough to be pliable, dust a work surface and a large plate with about ¼ cup cornstarch and coat your palms as well. Grab a large handful of mochi, roll it into a ball, and dip it in more cornstarch, rolling until it is not sticky anymore. Flatten the ball on the work surface using your palms to form a pancake that's about ¼ inch thick and at least 5 inches wide (if it's a little larger, that's fine).

Make sure the mandarins are well-dried before using. Place a mandarin orange upside down in the middle of the pancake, then bring the sides of the mochi up around the mandarin and pinch the dough together, sealing the fruit and removing any excess mochi dough to reuse for the next mochi ball. Place the mochi seam-side down on the plate sprinkled with cornstarch. Replenish the work surface and your palms with more cornstarch as needed, and repeat the process with the remaining mandarins.

If desired, poke a small hole in the top of each one and insert the stem of a mint leaf into each one as a garnish.

The mochi can be stored in an airtight container at room temperature for up to 2 days, but keep in mind that fresh mochi tastes better, and these are best eaten within 24 hours. If you do place them in the fridge, stale mochi can be revived by warming in a microwave on low power in short bursts, 5 to 10 seconds at a time.

Shortcut Spanish Rolls

½ cup panko bread crumbs

4 tablespoons (½ stick) salted butter, at room temperature

¼ cup packed light brown sugar

1 teaspoon vanilla extract

1 (8-ounce) can crescent roll dough

MAKES 8 ROLLS

Preheat the oven to 375°F.

Place the panko in a plastic bag and crush gently with a rolling pin (or pulse in a food processor) until it is less coarse, roughly the texture of fine bread crumbs.

Set half of the panko aside and add the remainder to a medium bowl, along with the softened butter, brown sugar, and vanilla. Mix with a fork until combined.

Open the crescent roll can and gently unroll the dough, separating it into 8 triangles. Spread a scant tablespoon of the panko-butter mixture edge to edge on one side of each triangle, then roll them up starting at the wide end. Roll each of the crescent rolls in the reserved panko until evenly coated, then transfer them to an ungreased baking sheet.

Bake until golden brown, 10 to 13 minutes. Serve warm.

A short drive from my home on Maui there's a Filipino bakery that makes incredible Spanish rolls, aka señorita bread, a soft, sweet bread rolled flat and filled with brown sugar and butter, then sprinkled with bread crumbs. (Nanding's on O'ahu does great ones, too.) A cousin of Mexican pan dulce, Spanish rolls are traditionally made from buttery brioche dough, but given how much they resemble your basic holiday crescent roll, there's a pretty obvious shortcut I like to use when making them: Pop open a can of crescent rolls and add the filling. The best thing about this low-commitment method is that it's easy to make a small batch in an instant, since the best way to eat Spanish rolls is warm from the oven, with a cup of coffee on the side.

Furikake Animal Crackers

24 ounces plain animal crackers

4 tablespoons (½ stick) salted butter

¼ cup sugar

1 tablespoon shoyu (soy sauce)

¼ cup agave syrup

¼ cup neutral oil

½ cup furikake (see Note)

SERVES 12

Preheat the oven to 250°F and position the racks in the upper and lower thirds of the oven.

Spread the animal crackers out over two large sheet pans.

While the oven is heating, in a small saucepan, melt the butter over medium heat. Add the sugar and shoyu and stir until the sugar is dissolved. Remove the pan from the heat and stir in the agave and oil. Pour the syrup over the animal crackers, then sprinkle on the furikake, using a silicone spatula or wooden spoon to stir the crackers until evenly coated.

Bake, stirring the animal crackers in each pan about every 15 minutes, until the crackers are golden and starting to brown around the edges, about 1 hour. Swap the sheet pans from top to bottom halfway through for even browning.

Let cool completely, stirring occasionally to keep the crackers from sticking together (they will look wet and soft when they come out of the oven, but will dry and harden as they cool). Store in an airtight container for up to 1 week.

My first cookbook had a recipe for furikake Chex mix that I was very proud of. Well, these are the next rung up on the snack ladder: animal crackers baked in a salty-sweet shoyu glaze and coated in sesame and nori. If you're shopping in Hawai'i, most everyone uses Diamond Bakery brand animal crackers, but if you're on the mainland, just use your favorite name brand (quality matters).

Note: I'm using a basic store-bought variety of furikake called nori fumi, which can be found in many supermarkets and contains just nori, sesame seeds, sugar, and salt. Don't worry if the furikake you have doesn't have the same exact name, as long as it has close to that combination of seasonings.

Pumpkin Crunch

For the cake

1 (29-ounce) can pumpkin puree

1 (12-ounce) can evaporated milk

1 cup packed light brown sugar

3 large eggs, slightly beaten

½ teaspoon ground cinnamon

¼ teaspoon ground nutmeg

1 (15-ounce) box moist yellow cake mix

1 cup chopped pecans

2 sticks (8 ounces) butter, melted

For the shortcut Chantilly cream (optional)

1 (3.4-ounce) box instant vanilla pudding mix

¾ cup whole milk

1 (8-ounce) container frozen whipped topping, thawed, or 3 cups whipped cream

SERVES 8

Preheat the oven to 350°F. Line a 9 × 13-inch baking pan with parchment paper.

Make the cake: In a large bowl, stir together the pumpkin, evaporated milk, brown sugar, eggs, cinnamon, and nutmeg until well combined. Pour the mixture into the lined baking pan.

Sprinkle the dry cake mix evenly over the pumpkin mixture, followed by the pecans. Spoon the melted butter evenly over the cake mix.

Bake until the cake is set and the top is golden brown, 50 to 60 minutes.

Let the cake cool in the baking dish. Once the cake is cool to the touch, refrigerate until ready to serve, up to overnight.

Meanwhile, prepare the Chantilly cream (if using): In a medium bowl, combine the pudding mix and milk and whisk until smooth. Gently fold in the whipped topping until no streaks remain. Place in the fridge until the cake is ready to serve.

When ready to serve, remove the cake from the pan and cut into squares. If desired, dollop with the Chantilly cream.

Shaved ice and malasadas are tough competition, but pumpkin crunch may be the most iconic dessert in Hawai‘i. A classic dump cake made with canned pumpkin, evaporated milk, pecans, cinnamon, yellow cake mix, and finished with whipped topping, it's the dessert that at least one kid brings to every end-of-year school potluck party. It's the kind of dessert that your relative who cooks the least will always make for a family gathering and cause everyone to remark, "*Oooh, they're the baker in the family!*"

The use of pumpkin and pecan might lead you to believe it's a seasonal dish, but this is a year-round dessert in Hawai‘i. Personally, I've been known to polish off a pan in one sitting. My recipe doesn't veer too far from the one you'll find printed on little index cards at the supermarket, except that I prefer to use a higher ratio of pumpkin puree for maximum custardy-ness.

Much like a slice of pumpkin pie, one of the long-running debates over pumpkin crunch is whether to serve it topped with cream or not. I love a dollop, but it's not a completely necessary addition. Standard whipped cream works fine, but for a local twist, try making it with shortcut Chantilly cream, which is whipped topping blended with vanilla pudding to give it some extra heft.

Guava Cheesecake

For the cheesecake

1 (12-ounce) block cream cheese, at room temperature

2 large eggs, slightly beaten

½ cup sugar

1 teaspoon vanilla extract

1 (9-inch) prepared graham cracker crust

For the topping

1 (12-ounce) can frozen guava nectar concentrate, preferably Hawaii's Own, thawed

1 tablespoon cornstarch

1 teaspoon unflavored gelatin powder

¼ cup warm water

1 tablespoon fresh lemon juice

SERVES 8

Preheat the oven to 350°F.

Make the cheesecake: In a medium bowl with an electric mixer, combine the cream cheese, eggs, sugar, and vanilla and beat on low speed until smooth. Pour the mixture into the prepared crust.

Bake until the filling is set, about 25 minutes.

Let cool completely.

Meanwhile, make the topping: In a small saucepan, bring the guava concentrate to a boil. In a small bowl, whisk together the cornstarch, gelatin, and warm water until dissolved. Stir into the guava concentrate. Reduce the heat to a simmer and add the lemon juice. Continue cooking, stirring frequently, until the topping is thick and clear, 1 to 2 minutes. Remove from the heat and let cool completely.

Once the guava topping has cooled completely, spread it over the cooled cheesecake. Refrigerate for at least 1 hour (and up to overnight) before slicing and serving.

This tangy tropical dessert is such a bakery fixture in Hawai'i, they even sell it at Costco. The perfect cheesecake is a divisive subject, but I've always felt they should taste more like cream cheese than cake. Hopefully you agree. The filling for this recipe is on the lighter, brighter side, with a short bake in the oven to set it in place. For the essential layer of tart-sweet guava jelly on top, use a can of guava juice concentrate from the freezer section. After it's thickened with cornstarch and chilled, it'll form a sweet, jiggly pink-red gel.

Vietnamese Coffee Swirl Brownies

Cooking spray or neutral oil, for the pan

For the condensed milk swirl

¼ cup boiling water

1 teaspoon instant espresso powder

1 (8-ounce) block cream cheese, at room temperature

¼ cup all-purpose flour

3 tablespoons sweetened condensed milk

1 teaspoon vanilla extract

For the brownies

¼ cup boiling water

1 tablespoon instant espresso powder

½ cup Dutch-process dark cocoa powder

8 tablespoons (1 stick) unsalted butter

½ cup granulated sugar

½ cup packed light brown sugar

2 large eggs

¼ teaspoon kosher salt

½ cup all-purpose flour

SERVES 8 TO 12

Preheat the oven to 325°F. Coat an 8 × 8-inch baking pan with cooking spray or oil.

Make the condensed milk swirl: In a small bowl, whisk together the boiling water and instant espresso until dissolved. Stir in the cream cheese, flour, condensed milk, and vanilla, and continue stirring until a smooth batter forms.

Make the brownies: In a mug or cup, whisk together the boiling water and espresso powder until dissolved. Add the cocoa powder incrementally, stirring, until a thick paste with no lumps forms. Set aside.

In a microwave-safe medium bowl, microwave the butter on low power until completely melted and warm, but not hot. Scrape in the cocoa-espresso paste and whisk until combined and let cool to room temperature.

Once the butter mixture has cooled, add both sugars, the eggs, and salt. Whisk until frothy. Add the flour incrementally, stirring, until the flour is incorporated and no dry streaks remain.

Scrape about three-quarters of the batter into the baking pan and spread into an even layer. Dollop the condensed milk mixture all over the brownie batter. Finally, dollop the remaining brownie batter over the top. Drag the tip of a knife across the top to swirl the layers together, just enough to form a cool pattern but not so much that they mix together.

Bake until the center is set, 25 to 30 minutes (if you are using a glass or ceramic baking dish, it may take longer). The brownies will pull away from the edges of the pan and a toothpick inserted into the middle will come out slightly moist with just a few crumbs.

Let the brownies cool completely in the pan on a wire rack before cutting and serving.

I'm not a pastry chef, but one thing I've learned working with them is that coffee somehow makes chocolate taste more chocolatey. My wife loves the strong flavor of dark chocolate, and I love the flavor of super-concentrated Vietnamese coffee, which is an easy way to drink what feels like seven shots of espresso in a single cup. The secret to these intensely chocolatey, extra-fudgy brownies is a combination of the two: dark Dutch-process cocoa powder and instant espresso powder (my favorite is the Café Bustelo brand), which yields a rich flavor and color that's balanced out with a swirl of cream cheese and condensed milk.

One reason I like making brownies over, say, cookies or cakes, is that although there's a little more work to make the batter up front, they're way easier not to overbake. The toothpick method is foolproof here: Near the end of the baking time, use a toothpick to poke the brownie in the center of the pan. When the toothpick comes out moist, but without any uncooked batter on it, it's good to pull.

Mango-Ade Cooler

¼ cup sugar (optional, if using frozen mango chunks)

2 cups chopped ripe mango (from 2 large mangoes) or frozen mango chunks

1 cup fresh orange juice

½ cup fresh lemon juice

Ice, for serving

Orange slices, for garnish (optional)

MAKES 6 CUPS

In a small microwave-safe bowl or coffee mug, combine the sugar and ½ cup water. Microwave for 2 minutes, then stir until the sugar has dissolved. Set aside to cool.

In a blender, combine the chopped mango and 3 cups water and blend until smooth. Depending on how fibrous the mangoes you're using are, you may need to strain the mixture through a sieve or cheesecloth.

In a large pitcher, stir together the mango juice, orange juice, and lemon juice. Add the cooled simple syrup and/or more water to taste (frozen mango chunks will generally be less sweet than ripe fresh mango). Serve over ice and garnish with orange slices, if desired.

Having too many ripe mangoes might only be a problem in places with tropical climates, but for locals with a mango tree in their yard, it's a challenge nonetheless. So when life gives you mangoes, make mango-ade. If you're using fresh ripe mango, you might not need much additional sweetener, but more simple syrup might be necessary if you're using frozen mango chunks, which tend to be more tart.

Cold Brew Soba Cha

½ cup raw buckwheat groats

Lemon slices (optional), for serving

Honey or your favorite sweetener (optional), for serving

MAKES 2 QUARTS

In a small saucepan or skillet, spread the buckwheat in a single layer and toast over medium heat, stirring constantly so that they brown evenly and don't burn. Once the kernels are fragrant and lightly browned, about 5 minutes, reduce the heat to medium-low and continue toasting until they turn a deep, rich brown color, another 2 to 3 minutes (you might start to hear popping sounds near the end as well).

Remove the pan from the heat and transfer the kernels to a heatproof bowl so they don't continue cooking in the pan. Toasted buckwheat can be stored in a sealed container in the fridge for up to 3 months.

Place the cooled buckwheat in a large glass jar or jug and cover with 2 quarts water. Place the container in the fridge and let it steep at least overnight and up to 24 hours. For a clearer, less cloudy tea, strain through a coffee filter before serving. Lemon slices and honey can be added to taste.

VARIATION

Single-Serve Hot Soba Cha: To brew a single portion of tea, pour 1 cup of boiling water over 1 tablespoon of toasted buckwheat. Brew for 5 to 10 minutes, depending on your preference, then strain and serve. (After straining, the soaked buckwheat can be added to hot oatmeal or cooked rice for an added nutty, toasted flavor—no need to cook it further.)

The older I get, the more I appreciate the power of a good beverage—something that I can sip all day in the kitchen to stay hydrated, but that isn't filled with sugar or caffeine, and is ideally a little more interesting than plain water. If you saw how many of my young line cooks start their shift by cracking a huge energy drink, you'd be amazed, but I'm happy those days are behind me.

Which brings me to soba cha, a kind of Japanese tea that isn't actually tea at all, but brewed from roasted buckwheat, the same seed used to make soba noodles (hence the name). Steep the kernels in water and you'll end with a caramel-colored tea that's toasty and nutty with a subtle bready sweetness despite having no sugar or caffeine.

Many Japanese stores sell soba cha, but the best part is that it's cheaper and just as easy to make your own using raw buckwheat groats, the kind found at any natural foods store or in the breakfast aisle. The only necessary step is to toast the buckwheat to give it a deep roasty aroma. After that, it can be brewed with cold water for iced tea, or with boiling water for hot. I like to brew a big batch in the fridge overnight, then strain it through a coffee filter so it's nice and clear. Soba cha is delicious with a little lemon and honey, but it's really best just plain. And if you want to be extra efficient, add the soaked toasted buckwheat (which doesn't need to be cooked and is full of nutrients) to a bowl of oatmeal or rice in the morning for nutty flavor and texture.

SAUCES & PICKLES

Ball
MASON

Shoyu Pickled Onions

½ cup shoyu (soy sauce)

½ cup apple cider vinegar or distilled white vinegar (or a mix)

½ cup sugar

½ cup water

2 medium sweet onions, cut into wedges and separated

3 cloves garlic, minced or grated

2 small hot chiles (optional), such as Thai or Hawaiian chiles, stemmed and lightly smashed

MAKES ABOUT 1 QUART

In a small saucepan, combine the shoyu, vinegar, sugar, and water. Bring to a boil, stirring constantly, then remove from the heat.

Layer the onions, garlic, and chiles (if using) in a 1-quart jar, then pour the hot pickling liquid over the top. If the onions aren't submerged in the brine, use a small stone or weight to press them down.

Let the jar cool completely on the counter for 2 to 4 hours, then place in the fridge for at least 2 days before eating. The pickled onions will last in the fridge for up to 1 month, but are at their best texture after 1 to 2 weeks.

Think of this as a nice stepping-stone into the world of Hawai'i pickles. It's originally a Korean dish, but without a doubt it's transcended cultures on the islands. We go through several gallons a week at Tiffany's and Tin Roof alone. The 1:1:1:1 ratio of shoyu, vinegar, sugar, and water (by volume) is easy to remember—the hardest part is patience. As the onions cure in the brine, they release their sweet oniony liquid and deepen the flavor of the pickle. They tend to be at their best after a week or so of pickling. As a pickle they will complement practically any dish, but I love them so much I usually just snack on them until the jar is empty.

White Kimchi

- 1 head napa cabbage (about 3 pounds)
- 5 tablespoons kosher salt
- ½ pound daikon radish (about ½ medium radish), peeled and julienned
- 1 small carrot, peeled and julienned
- ½ red bell pepper, julienned
- 3 scallions, cut into 1-inch lengths
- 1 medium Korean (Asian) pear or large sweet apple, peeled, cored, and roughly chopped
- ½ medium sweet onion, roughly chopped
- 8 cloves garlic, peeled but whole
- 2-inch piece fresh ginger, peeled and roughly chopped
- 1 tablespoon sugar
- ¼ cup fish sauce

MAKES ABOUT 2 QUARTS

Cut the head of cabbage lengthwise into quarters, then trim off the bottoms and cut into 2-inch squares. In a large bowl, sprinkle the cabbage with 4 tablespoons of the salt and thoroughly mix. Cover and let it sit in the fridge overnight.

The next day, rinse the cabbage in cold water a few times, then drain and return to the large bowl. Add the daikon, carrot, bell pepper, and scallions, tossing to combine.

In a food processor or blender, combine ¼ cup water, the pear, onion, garlic, ginger, sugar, and the remaining 1 tablespoon salt. Blend the mixture to a puree. Whisk in the fish sauce and pour over the salted cabbage. Mix thoroughly by hand.

Transfer the kimchi to an airtight container (or containers if you don't have one large enough), such as a clean glass jar or plastic container, gently packing the cabbage down (don't worry if the liquid doesn't completely cover the vegetables, it will rise over time), making sure there's at least 1 inch of headroom at the top of the jar.

Cover the jar or container loosely with a lid (sealing it could cause the fermentation gases to build up) and then drape a cloth towel over the top. Let it ferment at room temperature for 1 to 2 days, depending on your preferred sourness level (don't be shy about trying a piece after 1 day).

Transfer the kimchi to the fridge with the lid sealed and store for at least 1 week before eating. The texture will continue to change, and the kimchi will slowly become more sour over time. It can last up to several months in the fridge, but it's usually at its best after 3 to 4 weeks. If you see any mold or smell something off-putting, it's always best to discard.

White kimchi is a mild kimchi that's made without chile flakes, thus no heat. It does, however, still have those crispy, tangy, briny flavors you want from kimchi, with a mellow sweetness and brightness that comes from pear and ginger. What I like most about this style is that while it improves in flavor as it ferments, it's just as delicious when eaten fresh, or nearly fresh.

If you've got young kids who can't do spicy, having a jar of this kimchi in the fridge is a quick way to punch up school lunches or weeknight dinners, whether that's a bowl of fried rice or instant ramen. For a combination that's a little more grown-up, white kimchi with sashimi is an amazing pairing—the subtle funky flavors of the cabbage act as a seasoning for the fish.

Mustard Pickled Eggplant

2 pounds long thin eggplant (Japanese or Chinese work best)

2 teaspoons kosher salt

3 tablespoons shoyu (soy sauce)

2 tablespoons sugar

1 tablespoon rice vinegar

Juice of ½ lemon

1 tablespoon hot mustard powder, preferably Colman's

Finely chopped shiso or mint (optional), for serving

MAKES ABOUT 1 QUART

Cut the eggplant on the diagonal into ⅛-inch-thick slices. Transfer to a sheet pan and massage the slices all over with the salt. Put another sheet pan on top of the eggplant and weigh it down with heavy objects. Place in the fridge for at least 3 hours and up to overnight, draining off any liquid every hour or so as it collects.

When the eggplant slices are wilted and softened, add them to a 1-quart glass jar or other resealable container. In a small bowl, whisk together the shoyu, sugar, vinegar, lemon juice, and mustard powder. Pour over the eggplant, tossing to mix well. Place in the fridge and let marinate overnight (or several days if you have the patience), shaking occasionally.

Serve with chopped shiso (if using) on top. Any leftover pickles can be kept in the fridge for 2 to 3 weeks.

This spicy eggplant tsukemono is as old-timey as it gets in Hawaiʻi. You'd be hard-pressed to find a Japanese grandma over the age of eighty who couldn't make this with her eyes closed, or a grandpa who doesn't enjoying eating it once a week over a bowl of rice. I'm a big fan of this one because I usually associate eggplant with being soft and mushy, but curing the eggplant in salt and pressing out the liquid helps it stay crunchy and snappy even after marinating in hot mustard dressing. Enjoy with rice, or anything else that would benefit from a nose-clearing kick.

Black Sesame Butter

- 2 cups raw black sesame seeds
- ⅓ cup powdered sugar, plus more to taste
- ¼ cup peanut oil or other neutral oil
- 4 teaspoons toasted sesame oil
- 2 tablespoons maple syrup or agave syrup
- 1 teaspoon vanilla extract
- ¼ teaspoon kosher salt, plus more to taste

MAKES ABOUT 1½ CUPS

In a dry skillet, toast the black sesame seeds over medium-low heat, stirring regularly to toast evenly, until they start to smell nutty and you see little wisps of steam coming from the pan, 4 to 5 minutes. Remove the pan from the heat and let cool slightly (but not too much, the seeds blend most easily when they're still warm).

To avoid any spills, carefully transfer the warm seeds to a large measuring cup or other container first, then pour them in a food processor or blender. Add the powdered sugar and blend for about 30 seconds to 1 minute, until the mixture resembles gray sand. Add the peanut oil, sesame oil, syrup, vanilla, and salt. Blend again for another 2 to 3 minutes, scraping down the sides of the bowl about every 30 seconds, until the paste is similar to the consistency of natural peanut butter—not runny, but thin enough to stir easily. Taste and season with more salt or sugar as needed.

Transfer the paste to a lidded jar and store in the fridge for up to 1 month, or in the freezer for up to 6 months.

One of my chef heroes, Sean Brock, says the best chefs have the best pantries. This is the sort of condiment he's talking about. Think of it as a more sophisticated, less saccharine Nutella. It's sweet and rich enough to be used in desserts or eaten with toast (try a half-half mixture with fruit jam or cream cheese), but it's also earthy and nutty enough for savory applications where sesame paste, peanut butter, or tahini might be used. It also keeps for a long time. Since pure sesame oil is way, way too potent (and expensive), use a neutral oil to form the foundation of the buttery spread. I prefer peanut oil because it's widely available and the grassy flavor complements the sesame, but other extra-mild oils like avocado and grapeseed work, too.

Nori Salsa Macha

2 ounces large mild dried chiles, such as a mixture of guajillo and ancho, stemmed and seeded

½ ounce small spicy dried chiles, such as chiles de árbol or chiles japones, stemmed and seeded

3 (7 × 8-inch) sheets nori, or 3 packages nori seaweed snacks

1½ cups avocado oil, or other neutral oil

¼ cup unsalted dry-roasted peanuts

4 cloves garlic, sliced

3 tablespoons roasted sesame seeds, preferably black sesame seeds

1 tablespoon light brown sugar

1 teaspoon kosher salt, plus more to taste

2 tablespoons apple cider vinegar

1 tablespoon shoyu (soy sauce)

MAKES ABOUT 2 CUPS

Preheat the oven to 350°F.

Add the dried chiles to a baking pan in a single layer. Bake, stirring the pan once or twice, until the chiles are fragrant and puffed, 6 to 8 minutes. Remove the sheet pan and turn off the oven.

While the oven is still hot, place the nori sheets directly on the oven rack and bake them in the residual heat for 3 to 4 minutes, until they are crispy and brittle. (If you're using the nori seaweed snacks, arrange them on a wire rack or sheet pan before placing them in the oven.)

In a small saucepan, heat the avocado oil over medium heat until it begins to shimmer. It doesn't need to be smoking hot here. Add the peanuts, garlic, and sesame seeds to the oil and cook, stirring occasionally, until everything is fragrant and lightly browned, 2 to 3 minutes. Remove the pan from the heat.

Transfer the chiles, garlic, and nori to a food processor and pulse until finely chopped. Scrape the bottom and sides of the pan and add the warm oil mixture, the brown sugar, and salt. Pulse until combined. Add the vinegar and shoyu and pulse a few more times just to mix. Taste and season with more salt if needed.

Use immediately or transfer to an airtight container and store in the fridge for up to 1 month.

Salsa macha is an oil-based salsa made with dried chiles, various nuts and seeds, garlic, spices, and whatever else floats your boat. It's like Chinese chili crisp's Mexican cousin (or vice versa), and more to the point, it's punchy, smoky, and extremely craveable, adding excitement to whatever blank canvas on which it's heaped. Here, I'm expanding the original formula by adding umami-rich dried seaweed, which along with the dark dried chiles and black sesame seeds has the effect of creating a cool "midnight chili crisp" effect.

A crucial step here is oven-toasting a mixture of chiles—the larger ones add flavor, the smaller ones add heat—along with nori sheets so that they develop a deep earthy flavor and stay crisp once blended with oil. This can be done in a dry skillet, too, but it's easier to burn the chiles that way, and you don't want burnt chiles in your salsa macha.

If I'm eating this chili crisp it's perfect spooned on anything as is, but over boiled noodles you can thin it out with a little more vinegar and shoyu to taste to create an excellent and simple sauce for noodles.

Toyomansi

½ cup shoyu (soy sauce), plus more to taste

2 tablespoons fresh lime juice, plus more to taste

2 tablespoons fresh lemon juice, plus more to taste

Grated zest of 1 orange

Sugar (optional)

Freshly ground black pepper (optional)

MAKES ABOUT ¾ CUP

In a small bowl, stir together the shoyu, citrus juices, and orange zest until combined. The ratio can vary depending on your taste, but I usually go with roughly 2 parts shoyu to 1 part juice. Adjust with more shoyu or juice to achieve your preferred balance of salty and tangy flavors. You can also add a touch of sugar or pepper for a boost of flavor, if desired. Store in a sealed container for up to 2 weeks in the fridge.

Fellow Maui chef and Hawaiian waterman Issac Bancaco with his grandma May

This Filipino mother sauce is a straightforward mixture of toyo (soy sauce) and the juice of the sour-sweet fruit calamansi, balanced so the saltiness and citrusy tang are harmonized. Having made toyomansi in a lot of areas of the country where calamansi isn't readily available, I've found that equal parts lemon and lime juice with some orange zest added for fragrance gets you close to the real thing.

Since toyomansi is the Filipino cousin of ponzu, I use it in much the same way: mixed with olive oil for a simple salad dressing, as a finishing sauce for fish, or mixed with some combination of minced garlic, red onion, herbs, and/or chiles and used as a dip for meats or cooked vegetables.

Tomato Mango Chutney

3 tablespoons extra-virgin olive oil

1 tablespoon grated fresh ginger

1 teaspoon yellow mustard seeds

½ teaspoon gochugaru (Korean chile flakes) or red chile flakes

½ teaspoon fennel seeds

¼ teaspoon ground cumin

2 cups roughly chopped peeled plum tomatoes (about 4 medium tomatoes)

⅓ cup sugar, plus more to taste

¼ cup finely chopped sweetened dried mango

2 tablespoons minced garlic

2 jalapeños, seeded and finely chopped

½ teaspoon kosher salt, plus more to taste

MAKES ABOUT 2 CUPS

In a medium saucepan, heat the olive oil over medium heat until shimmering. Add the fresh ginger, mustard seeds, gochugaru, fennel seeds, and cumin. Cook, stirring frequently, for about a minute, until fragrant.

Stir in the chopped tomatoes, sugar, dried mango, garlic, jalapeños, and salt to the pan and bring to a boil. Reduce the heat to low and simmer the chutney uncovered, stirring occasionally, until the mixture thickens and the ingredients meld together, 20 to 25 minutes.

Taste and adjust the seasoning with more sugar or salt if needed. Remove the pan from the heat and let the chutney cool completely before transferring it to a lidded jar or other container for storage. Keep in the fridge for up to 1 month.

When I worked at Leoda's Kitchen and Pie Shop in West Maui, we would spread a generous layer of this sweet and zesty chutney on our popular ham and Cheddar sandwich. We used so much of it that we made it famous. The use of dried mango might seem counterintuitive in a fruit spread, but the sticky texture of dried fruit is what provides that jam-like consistency you want in a chutney. Beyond being a spectacular sandwich condiment, I also love it spooned onto pork chops and grilled chicken.

Mustard-Mayo Fry Sauce

½ cup yellow mustard, plus more to taste

½ cup mayonnaise, preferably Best Foods or Hellmann's, plus more to taste

½ teaspoon MSG or sugar, plus more taste

½ teaspoon garlic powder, plus more to taste

MAKES ABOUT 1 CUP

In a small bowl, stir together the mustard, mayo, MSG, and garlic powder until combined. Taste and adjust to your preference. Add more mustard for tanginess, mayo for creaminess, MSG or sugar for depth, or garlic powder for extra flavor. This keeps in the fridge practically forever.

When you go to a classic drive-in in Hawai'i—the kind with cheeseburgers, fried noodles, teri plates, and such—this is the classic dipping sauce. I don't think it even has a name beyond "mustard mayo." I enjoy it most as a fry dip, better than ketchup even! The added seasoning are the secret ingredients different spots use to make their sauce extra *ono*. Serve as a dip or sauce with fries, chicken nuggets, hot dogs, burgers, pickles, celery, cheese, pretzels—or anything else that goes well with creamy mustard.

Ginger Chimichurri

3 scallions, chopped

1 large shallot or ½ small red onion, chopped

3-inch piece fresh ginger, peeled and roughly chopped

3 cloves garlic, peeled but whole

1 serrano chile, seeded and chopped

½ cup roughly chopped fresh parsley

½ cup roughly chopped fresh cilantro

¼ cup roughly chopped fresh basil

2 tablespoons chopped fresh mint

2 tablespoons rice vinegar

1 tablespoon fish sauce

¼ cup extra-virgin olive oil

1 tablespoon toasted sesame oil

Kosher salt and freshly ground black pepper

MAKES ABOUT 2 CUPS

In a food processor, combine the scallions, shallot, ginger, garlic, serrano, parsley, cilantro, basil, mint, rice vinegar, and fish sauce. Pulse the ingredients until finely chopped. With the food processor running on low, slowly drizzle in the olive oil and sesame oil until the mixture is well combined and forms a sauce. Taste and season with salt and pepper. Keep in the fridge for up to 1 week.

Childhood friend and now pilot Alex Dalere with his wife, Kristin, and their kids

The elevator pitch for this zesty bright green condiment is that it's a cross between traditional chimichurri and Chinese ginger-scallion sauce, and just as useful as either of them. The quickest way to prepare it is to blitz everything in a food processor, but if you prefer the low-tech method, you can also use a mortar and pestle, or just finely chop everything on a cutting board. Use it as you would any chimichurri, which is to say as a condiment with grilled or roasted meats or as a dressing for vegetable dishes, a dip for bread, or any other way you can think up.

Double Hot Horseradish Mustard

3 tablespoons prepared horseradish

⅔ cup sour cream

⅓ cup mayonnaise

2 tablespoons Chinese hot mustard

Kosher salt and freshly ground black pepper

MAKES ABOUT 1½ CUPS

Drain the horseradish in a sieve, pressing out any remaining liquid. In a small bowl, whisk the drained horseradish, sour cream, mayo, and mustard together and season with salt and pepper to taste. Chill in the fridge for 20 minutes before serving. Keeps in the fridge for 2 to 3 weeks.

Longtime friend and Native Hawaiian designer and cultural practitioner Kuhao Zane, Native Hawaiian attorney Shae Kamaka'ala, and their daughter

This spicy, sharp, nose-clearing condiment is the definition of a double whammy. Mixing hot mustard and horseradish together combines two similar but distinct kinds of spiciness that build on each other in a way that I really enjoy. This recipe is for a cream-style horseradish sauce that goes well with prime rib or other meats, including hot dogs, but I also recommend mixing just the horseradish and hot mustard together and storing them in the fridge, then mellowing their kick with your preferred amount of mayo or cream to taste as needed.

Chile Vinegar

1 cup apple cider vinegar

¼ cup fish sauce

3 cloves garlic, smashed

3 to 4 small hot chiles, such as Thai or Hawaiian chiles, finely chopped

MAKES ABOUT 1½ CUPS

In a small twist-top jar, combine the vinegar, fish sauce, garlic, chiles, and 2 tablespoons cold water. Shake or stir to mix. The vinegar can be used immediately, but it will taste better after 2 to 3 days in the fridge, where it lasts indefinitely.

My cousin Tiffany (center) with her husband, Manny, and their children

Filipino sinamak is a spiced vinegar that you'll find in little bottles on practically every table in the Philippines. In Hawai'i it's referred to generally as chili vinegar, but as a condiment it's no less popular. Chile vinegar functions somewhere between a hot sauce and a squeeze of lemon, and it's no exaggeration to say it tastes great doused on everything—grilled meats, stewed vegetables, rice dishes, etc. If you don't have fish sauce on hand or are just looking to omit it, you can replace it with an equal amount of water and ½ teaspoon kosher salt, then adjust with more salt to taste.

ACKNOWLEDGMENTS

To my Janice, Chloe, Peyton, Quinn, and Asher, you are my heart, my purpose, my everything. All I ever want is to be the best husband and father for you.

To my coauthor, Garrett Snyder—I am forever indebted to you. Collaborating on two cookbooks has been an incredible journey, and I am continually amazed by the way you've taken our ideas and given them voice with such clarity and heart. Beyond the books themselves, I treasure the friendship we've built along the way. We've both grown and evolved so much since we first met, and I look forward to all that lies ahead.

Mahalo to the gifted photographer Kevin Miyazaki, whose artistic vision brought the storytelling of this book to life. From the moment I met you, I knew I wanted to work with you again—it has been such a joy to collaborate with someone so talented, kind, and easy to work with.

Mad props to prop stylist Melissa Padilla for capturing the spirit of ohana with such thoughtfulness and care. And to food stylist Chef Nolan, thank you for preparing every recipe with dedication and insight.

Thank you to the Clarkson Potter ohana for your patience, empathy, and unwavering support in bringing this project to fruition.

To my agent, Katherine Cowles, mahalo for your unwavering belief in me and for encouraging me to take on a second book. Had it not been for your support and steady cheerleading, I might never have attempted it. Your patience through my silences and your faith through my doubts mean more than I can say. I am deeply grateful.

To my dad, Reinior, and my brother, Jeremy—thank you for always being there for me and for always being "Down!" for whatevers. From cookbooks to restaurants, catering, events, and every project in between, you've had my back every step of the way. I couldn't have done it without you.

Mahalo to the Speeres, Chef Chris and Auntie Becky, for welcoming me into your Huelo home, a place of inspiration and creativity. Your mentorship, generosity, and the way you live with such heart and community inspire me, not only as a chef but also as a person. I am truly grateful to have you both in my life.

Mahalo to my family and friends for always being there, especially in moments when motivation was hard to find. Whether as listeners, taste testers, dishwashers, grocery getters, or simply by sharing your families and your time, your support and presence made this journey richer.

Mahalo to the people of Hawai'i. I am grateful for the privilege of sharing our home through this book.

With the photography team: Melissa Padilla, Nolan Gonzales, and Kevin Miyazaki

INDEX

Note: Page references in *italics* indicate photographs.

D

E

F

G

H

Clarkson Potter/
Publishers
An imprint of the Crown Publishing Group
A division of Penguin Random House LLC
1745 Broadway
New York, NY 10019
clarksonpotter.com
penguinrandomhouse.com

Library of Congress Cataloging-in-Publication Data is available at LCCN 2025017590.

ISBN 978-0-593-58102-5
eISBN 978-0-593-58103-2

Editor: Francis Lam
Editorial assistant: Darian Keels
Designer: Marysarah Quinn
Production editor: Christine Tanigawa
Production manager: Kim Tyner
Compositors: Merri Ann Morrell, Zoe Tokushige, and Hannah Hunt
Food stylist: Nolan Gonzales
Prop stylist: Melissa Padilla
Copyeditor: Kate Slate
Proofreaders: Eldes Tran, L. J. Young
Indexer: Ken DellaPenta
Publicist: David Hawk
Marketer: Chloe Aryeh

Manufactured in China

10 9 8 7 6 5 4 3 2 1

First Edition

The authorized representative in the EU for product safety and compliance is Penguin Random House Ireland, Morrison Chambers, 32 Nassau Street, Dublin D02 YH68, Ireland, https://eu-contact.penguin.ie.